D0616670

N8337F

AN ILLUSTRATED GUIDE TO
MODERN AIRBORNE
MISSILES

Bill Gunston

A Salamander Book

© 1983 Salamander Books Ltd.,
Salamander House,
27 Old Gloucester Street,
London WC1N 3AF,
United Kingdom.

ISBN 0 86101 160 0

Distributed in the United Kingdom by
Hodder & Stoughton Services,
PO Box 6, Mill Road,
Dunton Green, Sevenoaks,
Kent TN13 2XX

Contents

Credits

Author: Bill Gunston, former Technical Editor of *Flight International,* Assistant Compiler of *Jane's All the World's Aircraft,* contributor to many Salamander illustrated reference books.

Editor: Philip de Ste. Croix
Designer: Philip Gorton

Colour drawings:
Terry Hadler, Mike Badrocke, Wilf Hardy and Mike Trim
© Salamander Books Ltd

Line drawings: TIGA
© Salamander Books Ltd

Photographs: The publishers wish to thank E.C.P. Armées (page 81) and the other official international governmental archives, missile manufacturers and private individuals who have supplied pictures for this book.

Printed in Belgium by Henri Proost et Cie.

Air-to-Air

AAMs—air-to-air missiles—were first developed in World War 2. Early types had command guidance, with steering commands sent to them either along fine wires or via a radio link from the launching aircraft. By the 1950s the technology had moved on to more advanced guidance which enabled the AAM to home on its target, in other words to steer itself towards its target. The two favoured methods were SARH and IR homing, and they remain so to this day.

SARH, semi-active radar homing, requires the launching fighter to have a radar which can lock-on to the hostile aircraft so that the latter is caught in the radar's beam. It is said to be 'illuminated', just as if it were caught in the beam of a searchlight. The AAM is then fired, and its sensitive radar receiver in the nose, tuned to the fighter's radar signals, picks up the radiation which is scattered or reflected from the target and causes the missile continuously to steer towards their source. No matter how the hostile aircraft tries to escape, it is outmanoeuvred by the AAM until the latter either strikes it or has its warhead triggered by a proximity fuze as it flashes past.

IR, infra-red, today rivals radar in its general importance in warfare. IR, or heat radiation, is the same thing as radio or radar waves but with the difference that the wavelength is many times shorter

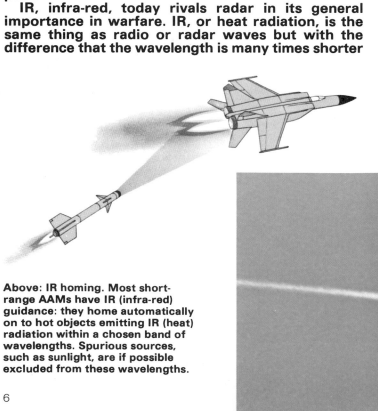

Above: IR homing. Most short-range AAMs have IR (infra-red) guidance: they home automatically on to hot objects emitting IR (heat) radiation within a chosen band of wavelengths. Spurious sources, such as sunlight, are if possible excluded from these wavelengths.

(almost as short as the visible waves we call light). To some degree this means that the AAM seeker head can be smaller, but the most important difference is that no illumination is needed; the target generates IR radiation itself. It would be hard to think of a better IR source than the combustor of a modern jet engine, but this is inside the engine and cannot be seen. The final turbine rotor stage and jetpipe are much cooler, but still a very powerful IR source, and 30 years ago there was no intrinsic problem in making a sensitive seeker that could steer a missile on to it.

At first IR missiles sometimes tended to home on the Sun, or on to its reflection in a friendly pond or greenhouse. In any case, while it is traditional for a fighter to get behind its enemy, it would clearly be more useful if an AAM could be made sensitive enough to detect and home on to the IR radiation emitted by a target aircraft in all directions. (This was doubly important to ground troops, whose first generation of IR anti-aircraft missiles had to wait until the hostile aircraft had made its attack and was departing before they would lock-on to the receding jetpipes!) Modern IR missiles have seekers of amazing sensitivity which not only lock-on at great distances, with the target aircraft in any aspect (even head-on) but also have much better performance through clouds and rain. ▶

Right: AIM-9L Sidewinder is a typical IR-guided AAM, with a body diameter of 5in (127mm). It needs little connection to the fighter apart from a launch rail, electrical firing socket and a cryogenic system to refrigerate the IR seeker.

Left: AIM-9L has an ABF (annular blast/fragmentation) warhead, triggered by a proximity fuze.

▶ Though AAMs are also carried by attack aircraft for self-defence, and even for the same purpose by such aircraft as the RAF Nimrod ocean patroller when in the South Atlantic, the usual carrier is, of course, the fighter. Most fighters are so-called dogfighters for close air combat, and their AAMs are small and very agile to kill at a range of a very few kilometres. But there also exists a class of larger aircraft, called interceptors, which have the ability to detect and destroy hostile aircraft at great distances from their home base, and even at great distances from themselves. For example the RAF Tornado F.2 has to protect all airspace from Iceland to the Baltic, no matter what the weather. Its powerful radar can select a target—even a small aircraft seen end-on—and lock-on to it at a distance of scores of miles. One AAM, the US Navy's Phoenix, can actually destroy its target at a range of over 100 miles.

Such high-performance missiles need to fly very fast, say Mach 4 (four times the speed of sound). This calls for a stainless-steel airframe (except for the radome, which has to be ceramic) and special streamlining. The motor, which in almost all AAMs is a solid-propellant rocket, has to have a very long burn time in order to keep up the speed. Close-range AAMs blast off with very high acceleration and then coast the rest of the way. As the speed bleeds off, so

does the power of manoeuvre fall away, and it is clearly central to every AAM to be able to out-manoeuvre all targets.

In many ways the AAM's task is easy. An aerial target stands out well in a large block of airspace and in a war situation any such target is worth a missile. This contrasts with the land battle, where out of thousands of moving vehicles only a few are high-value battle tanks, self-propelled guns, mobile missiles or anti-aircraft systems, which have to be picked out from the rest. But today's attack aircraft try to penetrate hostile airspace by flying as low as possible, where they are more difficult to track by defending radars. Seen from above, such aircraft are very close to the intense clutter (unwanted reflections of radar waves) from the ground. Only in recent years have AAMs become clever enough to home from above on to such prey.

Another recent trend is the use of small self-homing AAMs for the defence of relatively small and slow aircraft such as tactical helicopters and close-support aircraft. Such missiles have to lock-on their targets with no help from the launch aircraft, and depart cleanly from a launcher which may be hovering at zero airspeed. Most have been derived from the SAMs (surface-to-air missiles) used by infantry, usually fired from tubes with IR or laser homing.

Left: Though it was designed over 20 years ago the Hughes AWG-9 radar and AIM-54 Phoenix missile can kill over ranges exceeding 100 miles (161km), giving the US Navy F-14 Tomcat capability no other fighter can equal. The red dome under the radar is an IR/EO seeker.

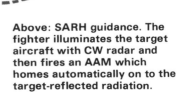

Above: SARH guidance. The fighter illuminates the target aircraft with CW radar and then fires an AAM which homes automatically on to the target-reflected radiation.

AA-1 Alkali

Origin: Soviet Union.
Propulsion: Solid motor with twin (left/right) sustainer nozzles.
Dimensions: Length 74in (1.88m); body diameter 7.5in (190mm); span 22.75in (578mm).
Weight: At launch about 200lb (91kg).
Performance: Speed, probably about Mach 1; range estimated at 5 miles (8km).
Warhead: Conventional, about 60lb (27kg).
Users: Retained in training and second-line units in Soviet Union and possibly East Germany.

So far as is known, this was the first AAM to go into operational use in the Soviet Union. Like all other known Soviet AAMs the original user was the PVO air-defence force. Development must have started around 1950, tailored closely to the parallel development of the somewhat crude interceptor radars grouped under the Soviet name of Izumrud. The earliest models of this radar known in the West are codenamed Scan Fix, and are said to have "fixed scan". This contradiction in terms is thought to mean that they are bore-sighted to point directly ahead, for ranging and target illumination for semi-active missile guidance. This primitive set was installed in the MiG-17P in the early 1950s, entering service by 1958. A few months later the gunless MiG-17PFU entered service with underwing racks for four of these early missiles. The associated radars are thought to operate in E/F-band. In contrast the missile next appeared on the MiG-19PM interceptor, associated with the later Scan Odd radar with alleged complex scanning patterns and operating in I-band at 9300-9400MHz. Like most Soviet AI radars this has two PRFs, around 900 pps for search and doubled frequency for tracking. This aircraft again carried

AA-3 Anab

Origin: Soviet Union.
Propulsion: Probably solid motor.
Dimensions: Length (IR) about 161in (4.1m), (radar) 157.5in (4.0m); body diameter 11in (280mm); span 51in (1.3m).
Weight: At launch about 600lb (275kg).
Performance: Speed about Mach 2.5; range (IR) about 12 miles (19km), (radar) at least 15 miles (24km).
Warhead: Unknown but probably large.
Users: Included East Germany (not operational), Soviet Union.

This second-generation AAM was the first large long-range all-weather missile to reach the PVO, which it did at about the time dummy examples were displayed carried by an early Yak-28P interceptor at Tushino at the 1961 Soviet Aviation Day display. At that time it was at first thought by the West to be an ASM, but gradually it was identified as a straightforward AAM carried in both IR and SARH versions, usually one of each. The carriers are the Yak-28P in all versions except trainers, Su-11 and Su-15. All these aircraft have the radar called Skip Spin by NATO, a much more capable installation than those associated with the earlier AAMs and probably derived from the Scan Three fitted to the Yak-25. Believed to be designated RP-11, it operates in I-band between 8690/8995 MHz at peak power of 200 kW, with a PRF of 2700/3000pps and pulse-width of about 0.5 microsec. It is assumed that CW illumination is provided for missile homing. AA-3 has large rear wings indexed in line with cruciform canard controls, and solid propulsion is assumed. Aerodynamics may be derived from AA-1, though as there appear to be no wing control surfaces it is probable that the canards can be driven as four independent units for roll control. There is no information on either type of homing head; the motor has

Above: Four early Alkali AAMs armed the MiG-19PM.

four launch rails apparently identical to those of MiG-17PFU and hung on prominent pylons. The third installation was the Su-9 all-weather interceptor, which again has the same four clumsy rails. This aircraft has yet another radar, called Spin Scan by NATO but believed actually to be designated R1L, and of a later family than the Izumruds. They operate in I-band, one version having over 100 kW peak and PRFs of 825/895 for search and 1750/1795 for track, with spiral scan. The missile is thus highly adaptable. It is

widely said to be radar homing and to manoeuvre by trailing-edge controls on the rear wings.

This is strange, because everything points to the following: beam-riding guidance, with coding to give automatic error-correction; control by the cruciform of nose fins; roll-stabilization by wing ailerons; and twin (lateral) motor nozzles well ahead of the streamlined boat-tail. There are at least six models of AA-1, some having cone/cylinder projections on the nose and all having fairings on the wingtips. The warhead is behind the canard controls. By 1978 all were thought to be withdrawn from combat units.

a single central nozzle, and may have boost/sustainer portions, and the warhead is amidships, with a proximity fuze. An AA-3-2 Advanced Anab has been identified since 1972, but how it is "advanced" has not become public. The Yak-28P is believed to have been withdrawn to reserve and training units, and the Su-11 is also gradually being phased

out of first-line PVO service, but this missile remains the primary armament of the Su-15 deployed in large numbers (1982 estimate, 700 in IA-PVO regiments excluding spares and reserves for attrition).

Below: All Sukhoi Su-15 versions carry AA-3 Anab missiles; this is a Flagon-D.

AA-2 Atoll

Origin: Soviet Union.
Propulsion: Solid motor resembling those used in Sidewinder, nozzle diameter 3.15in (80mm).
Dimensions: Length (IR) about 110in (2.8m), (radar) about 114in (2.9m); body diameter 4.72in (120mm); span (early AA-2 canard) 17.7in (450mm), (AA-2-2 canard and all tails) 20.9in (530mm).
Weight: At launch (typical) about 154lb (70kg).
Performance: Speed about Mach 2.5; range about 4 miles (6.5km).
Warhead: Blast-fragmentation, 13.2lb (6kg).
Users: Include Afghanistan, Algeria, Angola, Bangladesh, Bulgaria, China, Cuba, Czechoslovakia, Egypt, East Germany, Finland, India, Iraq, Jugoslavia, Laos, Libya, Morocco (stored), Mozambique, North Korea, Peru, Poland, Romania, Somalia, Soviet Union, Syria, Uganda, Vietnam, Yemen (both).

Unlike most Russian weapons this AAM is beyond doubt a copy of a Western original, the early AIM-9B Sidewinder. When first seen on 9 June 1961, carried by various fighters in an air display, it was almost identical to the US weapon. Since then it has followed its own path of development, and like Sidewinder has diversified into IR and SARH versions. Body diameter is even less than that of Sidewinder, and so far as is known all models have the nose-to-tail sequence of AIM-9B. The 13.2lb (6.0kg) warhead is a BF type with smooth exterior. Believed to be designated K-13A or SB-06 in the Soviet Union, several early versions have been built in very large numbers as standard AAM for most models of MiG-21, which carry two on large adapter shoes (which house the seeker cooling system in later models) on the underwing pylons. Licence production by the MiG complex of Hindustan Aeronautics has been in progress since the early 1970s, and it is believed there is also a Chinese version. Since 1967 there have been later sub-types called AA-2-2 or Advanced Atoll by NATO. Some reports ascribe these designations to the SARH versions, but the consensus of opinion is that there are IR and radar versions of the first-generation missiles, in

Above: The Libyan Arab Republic AF is a major user of Soviet AAMs, on three aircraft types. This Su-22 is carrying AA-2-2 Advanced Atoll AAMs.

various sub-types, and IR and radar versions of the Advanced model. Several photographs indicate that later models have quite different control fins. These fins are driven in opposite pairs through 30°, and the later fin is unswept, has a cropped tip and greater area and is fitted after loading on the launcher. Like AIM-9 versions, IR missiles have hemispherical noses transparent to heat, and radar versions slightly tapered noses that appear opaque. Current carriers include all later fighter MiG-21s, with four missile shoes instead of two, and the MiG-23S swing-wing fighter which also carries later AAMs.

Below: A US Navy portrait of a Libyan Flogger-E (MiG-23 export model) armed with four Advanced Atoll AAMs and a GSh-23 gun on the centreline.

AA-5 Ash

Origin: Soviet Union.
Propulsion: Probably solid motor.
Dimensions: Length (IR) 18ft (5.5m), (radar) 17ft (5.2m); body diameter 12in (305mm); span 51in (1.3m).
Weight: At launch about 860lb (390kg).
Performance: Speed about Mach 3; range (IR) about 13 miles (21km), (radar) about 35 miles (55km).
Warhead: Unknown but probably large, perhaps 100lb (45kg).
User: Soviet Union.

This large AAM was developed in 1954-59 specifically to arm the Tu-28P long-range all-weather interceptor, and genuine missiles were seen carried by a development aircraft of this family at the 1961 Aviation Day display at Tushino. (This aircraft had a very large ventral bathtub believed to house side-looking or early-warning radar, not seen subsequently). Early versions of Tu-28P, at first mistakenly reported as Blinder but corrected to Fiddler, carried two of these missiles on underwing pylons. So far as one can tell, they were SARH guided, associated with the Big Nose radar of the carrier aircraft, a very large and powerful I-band radar which had no counterpart operational in the West until the AWG-9 of 1974. The missile is matched to the radar in scale, being larger than any Western AAM.

Below: Artist's impression of a Tu-128 Fiddler interceptor in service with the Soviet PVO, armed with four Ash missiles. No other air-defence aircraft has such long radius of action.

Left: AA-5s awaiting loading on to a row of Tu-128 interceptors. Powered loading is essential for such large, heavy and delicate weapons, which can be rendered unserviceable by any severe impact or jolt.

Above: The IR (inboard) and radar (outboard) missiles under the right wing of a Tu-128. Like the photograph opposite this was taken from a Soviet propaganda film, hence the blurred reproduction.

For many years Western estimates of AA-5 range were ludicrously low, but they are creeping up and may now be about half the true value for the radar version.

Early Tu-28Ps are thought to have entered PVO service soon after 1961, filling in gaps around the Soviet Union's immense frontier. By 1965 the Tu-128 was being armed with the newly introduced IR version of this missile. This aircraft has four underwing pylons carrying the IR version, with Cassegrain optics behind a small nose window, on the inners and the SARH model, with opaque (usually red-painted) conical nose on the outers. Early versions of MiG-25 Foxbat interceptor were also armed with this missile, usually one of each type. It is not known whether these aircraft also had Big Nose or an early model of Fox Fire radar. This large but obsolescent weapon remains in the IA-PVO inventory as the standard armament of the Tu-128 Fiddler, the production aircraft, which (despite repeated rumours of an interceptor version of the Tu-22 Blinder) has no known replacement offering the same combat radius.

AA-6 Acrid

Origin: Soviet Union.
Propulsion: Unknown but probably solid motor with very long-burn sustainer.
Dimensions: Length (IR) 248in (6.3m), (radar) 232in (5.9m); body diameter 15.7in (400mm); span 88.6in (2.25m).
Weight: At launch (both) about 1,765lb (800kg).
Performance: Speed about Mach 4; range (IR) about 15.5 miles (25km), (radar) about 50 miles (80km).
Warhead: Unknown but US estimate 132-200lb (60-90kg), blast/fragmentation.
Users: Include Libya and Soviet Union, possibly Algeria and Syria.

Largest AAM in the world, this awesome weapon family was designed around 1959-61 originally to kill the B-70 Valkyrie (which instead was killed by the US Congress) and entered PVO service as definitive armament of the Mach 3.2 MiG-25 "Foxbat A" interceptor. With four missiles, two IR-homers on the inner pylons and two SARH on the outers, this aircraft is limited to Mach 2.8. (It is, of course, totally a straight-line aircraft at such speeds, and in its original form was not intended for any kind of close encounter with hostile aircraft. Since 1975 developed versions with many changes have emerged able to withstand about +6g at Mach 2 and armed with AA-6 and AA-7 missiles). Like the Tu-28, the MiG-25 was intended to detect targets at long range, using the Markham ground-air data link to give a cockpit display based on ground surveillance radars, switching to its own Fox Fire radar at about 100 miles' (160km) range. This equipment, likened to an F-4 AWG-10 in character but greater in power, includes CW aerials in slim wingtip pods to illuminate the target for the SARH missiles, which could probably lock-on and be fired at ranges exceeding 62 miles (100km); both peak-pulse/CW power and receiver-aerial size are considerably greater than for any Sparrow and closely similar to AWG-9/Phoenix. The IR version has much shorter range, though there is no reason to doubt that current Soviet technology is increasing IR fidelity as is being done elsewhere. Acrid has a large long-burning motor, giving a speed generally put at Mach 4 (the figure of 2.2 in one report is nonsense) and manoeuvres by canard controls, with supplementary ailerons (possibly elevons) on all four wings. The latter have the great area needed for extreme-altitude interception, for the B-70 cruised at well over 70,000ft (21km); but early Acrid missiles did not have look-down capability. Soviet films suggest that, when the range is close enough, it is usual to follow national standard practice and ripple missiles in pairs, IR closely followed by SARH. The two homing heads

Right: Two AA-6 Acrids on a Libyan MiG-25. The radomes appear bulged in this view.

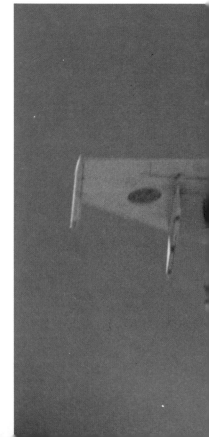

Above: The first MiG-25 air-to-air photograph, taken in 1974, showed early AA-6 missiles.

are different in shape, the IR head being a curved ogive and the radar type being a pointed cone. Despite reports that it is carried by the later versions of Su-15, no missile of this family has been seen on any interceptor other than the PVO MiG-25. Later versons of this aircraft are believed to carry the so-called AA-X-9.

AA-7 Apex

Origin: Soviet Union.
Propulsion: Advanced boost/sustain solid motor.
Dimensions: Length (radar, only known version) 181in (4.6m); body diameter (front) 7.7in (195mm), (main section) 8.8in (223mm); span 39in (1m).
Weight: At launch, about 705lb (320kg).
Performance: Speed about Mach 3; range (radar) estimated from 12.4 miles (20km) to at least 25 miles (40km).
Warhead: Unknown but one US report states 88lb (40kg).
Users: Include Czechoslovakia, East Germany, India, Libya, Soviet Union; probably increasing number of other countries.

Standard medium-range AAM carried on the glove pylons of the MiG-23 in all its interceptor versions, this missile is aerodynamically similar to the AA-5 Ash. The large cylindrical body rides on four large delta wings and four rear control fins indexed in line around the nozzle of the motor. The newer weapon is, however, somewhat smaller, and has a totally different front end. Curiously, the body diameter is reduced over almost the first metre from the tip of the nose, so the guidance section has to fit in a constricted portion. As in other Soviet AAMs there are believed to be IR and SARH versions, and while a smaller diameter may not reduce IR seeker performance it obviously must restrict the diameter of the receiver aerial in the SARH model. In fact, there may not be any SARH dish, because surrounding the guidance section are four projections which were at first wrongly identified by Western observers as extra control surfaces but which in fact are almost certainly SARH receiver aerials working on an interferometer principle (as do the four aerials spaced around the nose of the Sea Dart missile). It should be possible to home on the signals received by these four shallow fin-like projections, and dispense with the need for an internal radar dish. At the same time, the reason for the reduced diameter of the forebody of this missile is obscure, unless it is to provide an area-ruled ogival platform to carry the four blade aerials.

AA-8 Aphid

Origin: Soviet Union.
Propulsion: Advanced boost/sustain motor, probably solid.
Dimensions: Length (IR, only known version) 84.6in (2.15m); body diameter 4.72in (120mm); span 15.75in (400mm).
Weight: At launch about 121lb (55kg).
Performance: Speed about Mach 3; range estimated 0.3-3.5 miles (500m-5.5km).
Warhead: Estimated at 13.2lb (6kg).
Users: Include East Germany, India, Libya, Soviet Union; probably others including most MiG-23 users.

Supplementing and eventually probably to replace the vast stock of AA-2 Atoll close-range missiles, this interesting weapon is one of the smallest guided AAMs ever built, and is being produced in extremely large quantities as the air-combat missile of the PVO, FA and possibly AV-MF for the 1980s. Very similar in shape and size to the USAF Hughes Falcon of 30 years ago, AA-8 is a technically novel canard with delta wings right at the tail, canard delta control fins and, at the extreme nose and immediately ahead of the control fins, four rectangular blades of very low aspect ratio and with span considerably less than that of the controls. These are believed to be fixed aerodynamic surfaces to enhance combat manoeuvrability, but they are by no means obviously linked for this purpose with the movable fins as are the two sets of surfaces in the French Matra Magic missile, and it is possible that the fixed blades serve a different function

Above: MiG-23MF interceptor with AA-7 and AA-8 missiles.

Immediately to the rear, at the upstream end of the full-diameter section, a dark ring probably locates the windows of the proximity fuzing system. The warhead is estimated at no less than 88lb (40kg). The tail controls are cropped at the tips at an angle appropriate to about Mach 3, and carry near the tips forward-facing bullet fairings similar to those on the wings and control fins of certain other Soviet anti-aircraft missiles. The only really puzzling thing about AA-7 is its very poor Western estimated performance, which may simply be yet another case of rather childish wishful thinking. There is no evident reason why this missile should not have performance appreciably greater (in range, ceiling and manoeuvrability) than most versions of Sparrow, its nearest Western counterpart. The High Lark J-band radar of most MiG-23 interceptors is a set in the 150-kW class with a plate aerial of about 30in (0.76m) diameter. If the low estimates of AA-7 range are accurate, one explanation might be devotion of much of the missile body to duplicated guidance methods in each round, with extremely sophisticated ECCM circuits to ensure that the homing lock is never broken. The only alternative is a sharp upward revision of the estimated flight performance. AA-7 was probably developed in 1971-74.

concerned with guidance or ECM. The only known AA-8 has a hemispherical glass nose for an IR seeker, though some Western reports state that there is also an SARH model. Almost certainly AA-8 propulsion is of the boost/coast type, and it may have better manoeuvrability than any other AAM over ranges up to about 5 miles (8km). A black stripe between the guidance section and motor almost certainly locates the proximity fuze for the warhead, which has been estimated at barely half the size of the warhead carried by all current models of Sidewinder. AA-8 was first seen in the West in 1976 but no clear photograph appeared until 1981. It is carried by the MiG-21, MiG-23 (on body pylons), Yak-36MP and probably others.

Below: MiG-21bis with AA-8 (inboard) and AA-2-2 missiles.

New Soviet Missiles

AA-9

Not yet publicly associated with a NATO code-name, this large and advanced AAM is the primary weapon carried by Foxhound, the new-generation two-seat derivative of the MiG-25. No picture has yet been published of this missile, but it was said by Washington sources to have done well in prolonged look-down shoot-down tests in 1978 at Vladimirovka. Impressive simulated kills were scored against target RPVs simulating US cruise missiles flying at heights within 200ft (91m) of the ground, after acquisition by the Foxhound at heights from 20,000ft (6,100m) upwards. Maximum range is expected to be in the neighbourhood of 80 miles (130km).

AA-X-10

This Western designation has been published for a further new AAM which is probably to be carried by the MiG-29 Fulcrum or other advanced fighter. No details are available.

AA-XP-1

American designation for another alleged new Soviet AAM; described by *Aviation Week* as "All-aspect, look down, shoot down, IOC (initial operational capability) 1984". Range said to be 11 to 19 nautical miles (12.7-21.9 miles, 20.4-35.2km).

AA-XP-2

American designation for another alleged Soviet AAM; described by *Aviation Week* in same terms as XP-1 but with range estimated at 21.5 to 38 nautical miles (24.9-43.75 miles, 40.3-70.4km).

AA-X-?

Said by a Washington report to be a new Soviet dogfight AAM; no details.

Above: Hybrid (rocket/ramjet) propulsion for this Firebolt gives a cruise Mach number of 4, about right for the proposed AIAAM.

AAM-1

Almost a direct copy of Sidewinder AIM-9E, this AAM was developed in 1960-9 by Mitsubishi Heavy Industries for use by F-86F, F-104J and F-1 fighters of the JASDF. In 1969-71 a total of 330 rounds were delivered and these have subsequently been in the JASDF inventory alongside larger numbers of Sidewinders. AAM-1 is unofficially reported to be slightly smaller (102in, 2.6m) and lighter (154lb, 70kg) than most Sidewinders, and to have the modest range of 4.3 miles (7km).

Below: AAM-1 was extensively tested from F-104J and F-1 trials aircraft of the Japan Air Self-Defence Force.

AAM-2

Under development at Mitsubishi Heavy Industries from 1972 this was intended to succeed AAM-1 with all-aspect collision-course guidance using an IR seeker head by Nihon Electric. More than 60 development missiles were fired but the JASDF decided to adopt Sidewinder as its next AAM and AAM-2 was terminated in 1977. Mitsubishi Heavy Industries is now studying IR-AAM (see p.35).

AIAAM

Intended as a successor to AIM-54 Phoenix, the Advanced Intercept AAM is an in-house development by Raytheon which was revealed in the form of a one-third scale model at the US Navy League 1982 Convention. AIAAM has aircraft configuration, with one set of wings and tail controls for twist-and-steer manoeuvring. An inclined supersonic inlet under the belly feeds an advanced ramjet or hybrid propulsion system. One possible propulsion contractor is CSD, whose hybrid propulsion for another vehicle (Firebolt) is illustrated here; CSD also provides an integral ramjet for the Vought STM (Navy supersonic tactical missile) and ducted rockets for other missiles. AIAAM thus has a wide choice of propulsion methods (indeed a company other than CSD could be selected as propulsion contractor), and is hoped to lead the way to the air-to-air member of the planned new family of air-breathing supersonic missiles offering enormously enhanced range and sustained high power of manoeuvre. Guidance will include mid-course and, it is predicted, active radar terminal homing. The US Naval Weapons Center began a two/three-year technology validation programme in early 1982, with simulations intended to lead to hardware tests including trials with complete guided rounds.

AMRAAM

Origin: Hughes Aircraft, Missile Systems Group, USA.
Propulsion: Advanced internal rocket motor, details and contractor not yet decided.
Dimensions: Length 145.7in (3.7m); body diameter 7.0in (178mm).
Weight: At launch 326lb (148kg).
Performance: Speed probably about Mach 4; maximum range in excess of 30 miles (48km).
Warhead: Expected to be lighter than 50lb (22kg).
Users: To include USAF, USN, USMC, Germany (West) and UK (RAF and possibly RN).

Also called BVR (Beyond Visual Range) missile, the Advanced Medium-Range AAM is the highest-priority AAM programme in the United States, because AIM-7F is becoming long in the tooth and is judged urgently in need of replacement in the 1980s by a completely new missile. AMRAAM is a joint USAF/USN programme aimed at producing a missile having higher performance and lethality than any conceivable advanced version of Sparrow, within a package that is smaller, lighter, more reliable and cheaper. AMRAAM will obviously be matched with later versions of F-14, -15, -16 and -18 equipped with programmable signal processors for doppler beam-sharpening and with advanced IR sensors able to acquire individual targets at extreme range. The missile would then be launched automatically on inertial mid-course guidance, without the need for the fighter to illuminate the target, the final terminal homing being by a small active seeker. The task clearly needs a very broad programme to investigate not only traditional sensing and guidance methods but also new ones such as target aerodynamic noise, engine harmonics and laser scanning to verify the external shape and thus confirm aircraft type. Multiple-target and TWS will be needed, and AMRAAM will have a high-impulse motor giving rapid acceleraton to a Mach number higher than 4, with subsequent manoeuvre by TVC and/or tail controls combined with body lift, wings not being needed. The original list of five competing groups was narrowed to two in February 1979, and at the end of 1981 Hughes was picked over Raytheon to build 94 test missiles, with options on 924 for inventory plus follow-on production (which, because the US buy alone is expected to exceed 13,000 for the USAF and 7,000 for the Navy/Marines, is expected to be split between two

Above: One of the 94 test AMRAAMs ready for firing from a Navy F-14A at Point Mugu.

contractors, Raytheon probably becoming second-source). By late 1982 the AMRAAM (always pronounced as a word) was well into firing trials with fully guided rounds doing well against increasingly tough targets at Holloman and Pt Mugu. Mid-course guidance is Nortronics inertial, and the small Hughes active terminal radar now uses a TWT (travelling-wave tube) transmitter. In 1980 West Germany and the UK signed a memorandum of understanding as-

signing AMRAAM to the USA and ASRAAM to the two European nations. Since then work has gone ahead on integrating the US missile into the RAF Tornado F.2, replacing Sky Flash, and the Luftwaffe F-4F (the latter possibly being refitted with APG-65 or improved APG-66 radar under the Peace Rhine programme). The Tornado Foxhunter radar may need a small L-band transmitter to provide mid-course updating. Testing of full-scale development rounds is due in 1984.

Below: Launch in spring 1981 of an AMRAAM test missile from an F-16A of the USAF. The wingtip missile is an AIM-9J.

Asalm

The Advanced Strategic Air-Launched Missile (also p.88) has since 1974 been one of the larger research programmes of USAF Systems Command, and the eventual vehicle was envisaged as not only a BDM (Bomber Defense Missile) but also an offensive delivery vehicle capable of flying many kinds of mission. In its primary role Asalm was to be carried in multiple by a strategic bomber and would be compatible with SRAM and cruise-missile pylons or rotary launchers. Triggered and launched automatically by the bomber's defence system, with radar and IR coverage at least over the entire rear hemisphere, the missile would quickly "air slew" (ie change course) to the desired heading to intercept the detected threat. Propulsion would be by an advanced ram-rocket giving high launch acceleration at all altitudes and sustained propulsion for a flight of more than 100 miles (161km). Cruising speed would probably be about Mach 4, rendering wings unnecessary. There would be "a sophisticated guidance system, low radar and IR signatures and sustained high-g maneuver capability". The warhead would be nuclear. McDonnell Douglas and Martin Marietta have been engaged in technology integration and flight-dynamics studies, while CSD and Marquardt work on the propulsion system. The Asalm (pronounced as a word) was to have been carried by the B-1B, B-52 and FB-111A, but in

Asat

For many years small offices within the US Department of Defense and USAF have studied Asat (anti-satellite) weapon systems. In 1979 these at last led to a programme for operational hardware, with a $78.2 million contract award by the USAF to Vought Corporation for an Asat system to be deployed by about 1985. It will comprise an advanced interceptor vehicle with guidance so accurate that it will destroy its targets by collision, no warhead being necessary. It will be launched by an F-15 aircraft (presumably following a pre-directed flight trajectory) and then boosted to orbital height by two rocket stages. The first stage is based on the SRAM (see SRAM entry, p.136), a Boeing Aerospace product, and Boeing will develop this stage, provide integration services and manage development of the mission control centre. The second stage will be Altair III, the Thiokol motor which for many years has been the fourth stage of Vought's Scout vehicle. McDonnell Aircraft will modify the F-15 to serve as the launch platform. An $82.3 million contract was voted in 1980 and a further $268 million in 1981 to continue development through flight testing in 1984.

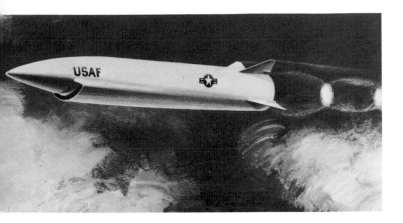

1980 the USAF decided not to proceed with it as a weapon for the inventory. It has since been a propulsion-technology demonstrator programme.

Above: An artist's impression of Asalm, showing the wingless body-lift configuration. It is extremely doubtful that development will be completed.

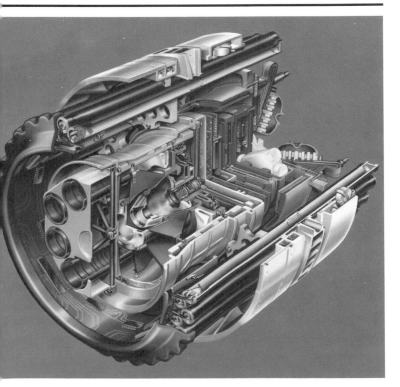

Left: Artist's portrayal of Asat launch from an Air Force F-15. The fighter acts merely as a launch pad, with guidance from ground stations only.

Above: This Vought interceptor has direct side thrust in any direction from 56 motors whose nozzles form a radial ring round the mid-section.

Aspide

Origin: Selenia Industrie Elettroniche Associate SpA, Italy.
Propulsion: Solid motor developed from Rocketdyne Mk 38 by Difesa e Spazio.
Dimensions: Length 12ft 1½in (3.7m); body diameter 8in (203mm); wing span 39.37in (1.00m).
Weight: At launch 485lb (220kg).
Performance: Speed Mach 4; range 31-62 miles (50-100km).
Warhead: Difesa e Spazio 72.75lb (33kg) fragmentation.
Users: Italy.

Though a wholly Italian development, and the largest single missile programme in the country, this impressive weapon was designed 'to be compatible with systems using Sparrow. This extends to AAM applications, for which the immediate prospect is the Italian Air Force F-104S Starfighter originally tailored to AIM-7E, and several surface-launched applications. The Italian SAM system using this missile is named Spada in its mobile land form; a different ship-to-air system is named Albatros. Similar to Sparrow in basic configuration, Aspide is powered by an advanced single-stage motor by SNIA-Viscosa Difesa e Spazio (which made the motors for Italian Sparrows) giving higher thrust and a speed of Mach 4 at burnout. The all-round performance is claimed to exceed that of even AIM-7F, and the guidance is likewise claimed to have significant advantages over that of the American missile. Matched with an I-band monopulse fighter radar, it is said to have greater ECCM capability, to offer increased snapdown performance and to be markedly superior at very low altitudes. The seeker aerial system is driven hydraulically. The radome and forebody are described as redesigned for more efficient operation at hypersonic speeds, and in the AAM role the moving wings are said to have extended tips with greater span. The fragmentation warhead is ahead of the wings. Following carry-trials in 1974 and prolonged static testing of the seeker, firing trials at Salto di

Below: Four frames from a ciné film taken during trials on the Salto di Quirra missile range on Sardinia, showing a Aspide with telemetry in place of a live warhead actually striking an Aérospatiale CT.20 target drone. The grey trail is kerosene.

1

2

3

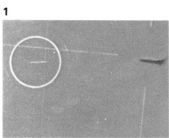

4

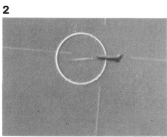

Quirra, Sardinia, began in May 1975. By 1977 fully representative Aspide missiles, including the AAM version, had completed qualification firings and production began in 1978. Final verification trials took place in 1979-80. The AAM is replacing Sparrow in the Italian Air Force and will also be a possible missile for Italian Tornados.

Below: Launch of an early Aspide missile from a box-type launcher at the Salto di Quirra range. Aspide is designed to be interchangeable with Sparrow and to be used as an alternative on aircraft, on ship launchers and even in land SAM systems. The only known carrier aircraft is the F-104S.

Asraam

Origin: UK/German consortium led by British Aerospace Dynamics and Bodenseewerk Gerätetechnik, (BGT).
Propulsion: Advanced solid motor, not yet defined.
Dimensions: Not defined but probably smaller than Sidewinder.
Weight: Probably lighter than typical Sidewinder.
Performance: Range limits probably to be about 0.6-9.3 miles; (1 to 15km) speed over Mach 3.
Warhead: Probably small, see text.
Users: Probably to include West Germany, UK, USA and most other NATO countries initially.

The obvious need for a completely new close-range AAM was made more acute by the progressive obsolescence of the AIM-9 family and cancellation of the German Viper and British SRAAM. After years of talking, the decision was taken at Government level to develop an Asraam (said as a word, the acronym meaning Advanced Short-Range AAM) in Europe for use by NATO. The MoU (memo of understanding) was signed by the USA, France (which has merely a watching brief), the UK and Federal Germany. Following a "pre-feasibility" stage which lasted to the end of 1981 the three actively participating governments authorized BAe Dynamics and BGT, the team leaders, to proceed to the feasibility study stage, which is expected to last into 1983. Project definition will extend into 1984, with engineering development lasting from 1985 to 1990 and production deliveries beginning "in the early 1990s". Clearly, the official view is that time and the effects of sustained inflation do not matter, and that Sidewinder can meet all challenges for another decade! Though US industry has no share in programme management it can bid at all stages, and is almost certain to play a major role in the eventual weapon. An excellent move was the invitation, accepted in September 1982, for Hughes to join the team to smooth compliance with US requirements. A severe, and seemingly unnecessary, handicap is that Asraam must fit launchers already in use for Sidewinder and Magic, even though the latter have large external controls and tailfins, while Asraam relies on body lift. Midcourse guidance could be by a simple strapdown inertial

Right: Asraam is potentially a vitally important missile which (whatever its partners may fail to do) BAe Dynamics must develop with the highest priority.

unit, giving greatly extended range especially in adverse weather. Terminal homing is expected to be by a staring focal-plane array IR seeker, all processing being digital by microminiature electronics. Nothing has yet leaked out regarding possible use of active radar homing, which could certainly be accommodated within a body diameter slimmer than Sidewinder. It might even be possible for each round to use both IR and active radar. The West has in the past lacked the Soviet Union's ability to select either type of guidance to suit prevailing weather. Objectives include minimum cost, zero maintenance over a long shelf life, all-aspect engagement and high kill probability with accuracy sufficient for direct-hitting to be guaranteed, eliminating need for a proximity fuze or large warhead. A possible configuration was shown in triple mockups on a single Sidewinder launcher at the 1982 SBAC show at Farnborough. One of the encouraging aspects of the programme is that, should development appear to lag, the USA could withdraw and produce its own Asraam; this should be a powerful incentive.

Falcon

Origin: Hughes Aircraft; some models licensed to Saab-Scania of Sweden.
Propulsion: Solid motor (various suppliers), some with boost/sustain charges.
Dimensions: See separate table of variants.
Weight: See separate table of variants.
Performance: See separate table of variants.
Warhead: Various 29-40lb (13-18kg) with proximity fuze (AIM-26A, 1.5kT nuclear).
Users: Canada, Finland, Greece, Japan, Sweden, Switzerland, Taiwan, Turkey, USA (AF, ANG).

First guided AAM in the world to enter operational service, Falcon was created with impressive assurance by a new team. In 1947 the newly created USAF asked for bids on a completely new radar-based fire-control system for manned interceptors, and a guided AAM for the following interceptor generation. To the surprise of most bidders both packages were won by Hughes Aircraft, lately diversified into advanced technologies and at that time of daily concern to Howard Hughes himself. By 1955 the family of fire-control systems had included the E-9, fitted to the F-89H, with a new computer and software for guns, FFARs or guided missiles. Subsequently the more advanced MG-10 followed for the supersonic F-102, the MG-13 for the F-101 and the semi-automated MA-1 for the F-106. All were matched to the missile Hughes created, at Culver City, and put into production at a new plant at Tucson in 1954. Called

Project Dragonfly, and at first classed as an experimental fighter (XF-98, see table), it matured as GAR-1 Falcon, but was later re-styled AIM-4, and for clarity the 1962 designations will be used throughout.

AIM-4 was an amazing exercise in packaging. The airframe, about the size of a man, contained a large proportion of GRP construction. Accelerated at about 50g by a single-charge Thiokol solid motor, it had a hemispherical nose radome flanked by receiver aerials like small nose fins, giving SARH proportional navigation and steering by elevons on the trailing edges of the slender-delta wings. Most early installations were internal, three being housed in the tip pod on each wing of the F-89H and J and six fitting the weapon bay of the F-102A. Both reached IOC with Air Defense Command in mid-1956. Later that year the first IR Falcon, AIM-4B, entered service with a distinctive glass nose, followed by AIM-4A (radar) with improved manoeuvrability from larger controls carried well behind the wings. AIM-4C had a better IR seeker able to lock-on against a wider range of ambient (background) temperatures. The IR missiles were especially popular in permitting the interceptor to break away as soon as the missile(s) had been launched

Right: One of the few remaining Falcon users is Sweden's Flyg-vapen. This J35F Draken interceptor has two HM-55s under the body and two HM-58s under the wing (see table for designations).

The Falcon Family

1947	1950	1962	Export	Sweden	Guidance	Length	Diameter
XF-98	GAR-1	AIM-4	—	—	SARH	77.8in (1.97m)	6.4in (163mm)
—	GAR-1D	AIM-4A	—	—	SARH	78.0in (1.98m)	6.4in (163mm)
—	GAR-2	AIM-4B	—	—	IR	79.5in (2.02m)	6.4in (163mm)
—	GAR-2A	AIM-4C	HM-58	RB 28	IR	79.5in (2.02m)	6.4in (163mm)
—	GAR-2B	AIM-4D	—	—	IR	79.5in (2.02m)	6.4in (163mm)
—	GAR-3	AIM-4E	—	—	SARH	86.0in (2.18m)	6.6in (168mm)
—	GAR-3A	AIM-4F	—	—	SARH	86.0in (2.18m)	6.6in (168mm)
—	GAR-4A	AIM-4G	—	—	IR	81.0in (2.06m)	6.6in (168mm)
—	XGAR-11	XAIM-26	—	—	SARH	84.0in (2.13m)	11.0in (279mm)
—	GAR-11	AIM-26A	—	—	SARH	84.25in (2.14m)	11.0in (279mm)
—	GAR-11A	AIM-26B	HM-55	RB 27	SARH	81.5in (2.07m)	11.4in (290mm)
—	GAR-9	AIM-47A	—	—	SARH/IRTH	126.0in (3.2m)	13.2in (335mm)
—	—	XAIM-4H	—	—	ALH	c80in (2.03m)	6.6in (168mm)

(though, as in the Soviet Union, it was common doctrine to fire one missile with each type of guidance to ensure a kill). These early Falcons accounted for three-quarters of the total production.

Above: On display outside the Tucson plant are (from left): AIM-4G, 4A, 4F, 4C, 26A and (foreground) 4D. Later Western AAMs gave up offering a ▶ choice of radar or IR guidance.

Span	Launch wt	Speed	Range	Production	
20.0in (508mm)	110lb (50kg)	M2.8	5 miles (8 km)	4,080	
20.0in (508mm)	120lb (54kg)	M3	6 miles (9.7 km)	12,100	
20.0in (508mm)	130lb (59kg)	M3	6 miles (9.7 km)	16,000	
20.0in (508mm)	134lb (61kg)	M3	6 miles (9.7 km)	13,500 (inc. 1,000 HM and	
20.0in (508mm)	134lb (61kg)	M4	6 miles (9.7 km)	4,000	3,000 RB)
24.0in (610mm)	150lb (68kg)	M4	7 miles (11.3 km)	300	
24.0in (610mm)	150lb (68kg)	M4	7 miles (11.3 km)	3,400	
24.0in (610mm)	145lb (66kg)	M4	7 miles (11.3 km)	2,700	
24.4in (620mm)	200lb (91kg)	M2	5 miles (8 km)	c100	
24.4in (620mm)	203lb (92kg)	M2	5 miles (8 km)	1,900	
24.4in (620mm)	262lb (119kg)	M2	6 miles (9.7 km)	2,000 (inc. 400 HM and	
33.0in (838mm)	800lb (363kg)	M6	115 miles (213 km)	c80	800 RB)
24.0in (610mm)	160lb (73kg)	M4	7 miles (11.3 km)	c25	

▶ In 1958 deliveries began of AIM-4E, the first so-called Super Falcon, to meet the greater demands of the F-106A. It introduced a longer-burning motor, advanced SARH guidance with a new receiver behind a pointed radome of new material, long wing-root fillets and a more powerful warhead. In May 1959 the Tucson plant switched to the -4F with a new motor having boost/sustainer charges, improved SARH guidance with greater accuracy and specific ECCM provision, and airframe modifications including a white moistureproof sleeve over the forebody and a 4in (102mm) metal probe on the nose to form a weak oblique shock and improve aerodynamics. A few weeks later came AIM-4G with the -4F airframe and a new IR seeker able to lock-on to smaller targets at considerably greater ranges.

In 1960 came a dramatic development. AIM-26 was developed to give high SSKP in head-on attacks. IR was judged inadequate in such engagements, and because of the reduced precision of SARH it was decided to use a much more powerful warhead. AIM-26A was fitted with almost the same nuclear warhead as Genie, triggered by four active-radar proximity-fuze aerials almost flush with the body ahead of the wings. The body naturally had to be of greater diameter, and a larger motor was necessary to achieve the required flight performance. AIM-26B followed, with large conventional warhead, and this was exported as HM-55 and licence-built by Saab-Scania as RB 27. Today about 800

Firestreak

Origin: DH Propellers, now British Aerospace Dynamics Group, UK.
Propulsion: Solid motor amidships with tube to nozzle.
Dimensions: Length 125.5in (3.188m); body diameter 8.75in (222mm); span 29.4in (746.8mm).
Weight: At launch 300lb (137kg).
Performance: Speed about Mach 3; range 0.75-5 miles (1.2-8km).
Warhead: Conventional 50lb (22.7kg) with IR proximity fuze system.
Users: Few remain with Saudi Arabia, UK (RAF).

Originally codenamed Blue Jay, this was the first guided missile of British origin to reach IOC, in 1958. Development began seven years previously, the prime contractor (de Havilland Propellers) being assisted by the RAE, RRE and RARDE, and with Mullard playing a central role in the IR guidance. Guided rounds were fired from 1954, a unique result being such an unbroken string of total successes that the team at first learned nothing (later the programme became more normal!). In 1955 a Venom launched a pre-production Blue Jay against a Firefly U.9, and about 100 rounds were then fired at the WRE from Avon-Sabres against

Jindiviks. In 1958 the missile was named Firestreak, and in Mk 1 form entered service with the Sea Venoms of 893 Sqn RN (two missiles), followed by the Javelin FAW.7 (four) with 33 Sqn RAF in August 1958. Subsequently various subtypes served with the Sea Vixen FAW.1 and 2 of the RN (four) and all marks of Lightning (two) of the RAF, Saudi Arabia and Kuwait. Several thousand rounds were produced, ending in 1969, and a few remain operational with Lightning users. The layout was very back-to-front. The aircraft equipment varied considerably, and in the Venom and Sabre was in an external bulge. Operational interceptors had a slaving unit which pointed the IR seeker head's Cassegrain telescope to look at the target held by the fighter's radar. Another unique feature was the eight-sided glass nose, like a sharp pencil. Error signals commanded proportional navigation by very small tail controls driven by long push/pull rods from actuators

Right: BAe Dynamics Firestreak seen on a Lightning of RAF No 74 Sqn (the first user of this interceptor). Both the missile and this F. Mk 3 aircraft are now withdrawn and in storage.

of the -26B model are the only Falcons left in USAF Aerospace Defense Command service. The Swiss Flugwaffe uses the HM-55 on the Mirage III-S, matched with Hughes Taran radar.

In 1958 Hughes began work on a challenging fourth-generation fire-control and AAM system to arm the Mach 3.2 "Zip-fuel" North American F-108 Rapier interceptor. The ASG-18 radar was used for mid-course guidance and target illumination over ranges exceeding 100 miles (161km), and the missile, then called GAR-9, was also given IR terminal homing. Propulsion was by a Lockheed Propulsion Co storable liquid rocket giving hypersonic speed, so that the wings became mere strakes along the body. In 1959 this very large AAM, still called Falcon, was transferred to the proposed YF-12A "Blackbird" research interceptor with which it conducted much basic fact-finding in advanced interception techniques.

The final production Falcon was the AIM-4D of 1963. The only Falcon tailored for anti-fighter combat, it was a crossbreed combining the small airframe of early models with the powerful motor and advanced IR seeker head of the large -4G. The result is a very fast and effective short-range missile. More than 8,000 -4A and -4C have been remanufactured to this standard. In 1969 the AIM-4H was funded to improve the -4D by fitting an AOPF (Active Optical Proximity Fuze) with four laser pancake beams at 90° to the major axis. It was abandoned for budgetary reasons in 1971.

in the forebody fed with air from a toroidal bottle near the motor nozzle! The air also drove a turbo-alternator. The seeker cell and potted electronics were cooled by nitrogen from the fighter. Nearing the target, two rings of IR sensors located behind glass windows ahead of the wings locked-on to the target to form a two-beam proximity fuze feeding target bearing and range and, at the correct point, detonating the 50lb (22.7kg) warhead surrounding the motor tube just ahead of the fins. Firestreak eventually achieved an SSKP of 85 per cent when fired within a 10,000ft (3050m) radius hemisphere to the rear of the target.

Genie, AIR-2A

Origin: Douglas Aircraft Co, USA.
Propulsion: Thiokol solid motor, 36,600lb (16,600kg) thrust.
Dimensions: Length 116in (2946mm); body diameter (except warhead) 17.5in (445mm); span (fins extended) 40in (1016mm).
Weight: At launch 822lb (373kg).
Performance: Speed Mach 3.3; range 5-6.2 miles (8-10km).
Warhead: 1.5 kiloton nuclear.
User: USA (AF).

Though it is an unguided rocket, which flies a near-ballistic trajectory, this can certainly be classed as an AAM and the most powerful in the world because it has a nuclear warhead. Development was begun by Douglas Aircraft in 1955, as soon as LASL (Los Alamos Scientific Laboratory) could predict complete success with the special 1.5kT warhead. The first live missile was fired from an F-89J at 15,000ft (4572m) over Yucca Flat, Nevada, on 19 July 1957. The rocket was detonated by ground command, and USAF observers standing unprotected at ground zero (ie directly under the burst) suffered no ill effects. During development this programme was called Ding Dong and subsequently High Card; its original designation was MB-1, changed in 1962 to AIR-2A. A training missile, with a white-cloud spotting charge instead of a warhead, was called Ting-a-Ling and is now ATR-2A. Genie is carried externally by the CF-101B and internally by the F-106, having earlier also armed the F-89J and F-101B. The Hughes MA-1, MG-10 or MG-13 fire-control tracks the target, assigns the missile, commands the pilot to arm the warhead, fires the missile, pulls the interceptor into a tight turn to escape the detonation, and finally triggers the warhead at the correct moment. Lethal radius is over 1,000ft (several hundred metres). Missile propulsion is by a Thiokol TU-289 (SR49) motor of 36,600lb (16,602kg) thrust. Flick-

HATCP

Origin: SA Matra, France.
Propulsion: SEP high-impulse solid motor.
Dimensions: Length 71.26in (1810mm); body diameter 3.54in (90mm).
Weight: At launch 38lb (17.3kg).
Performance: Speed Mach 2.6; range 0.3-3.7 miles (0.5-6km).
Warhead: Blast plus tungsten balls, 6.5lb (2.95kg).
User: Not yet developed.

Since 1981 the aggressive French Matra company has been promoting its SATCP surface-to-air weapon system in other roles, one of these being as an AAM for the augmentation of the weapon fit on helicopters and low-performance tactical aircraft of other kinds. The acronym HATCP derives from "hélicoptère/air très courte portée" (helicopter-to-air very short range). The missile is basically the same as in the SATCP system, except that the propulsion system may later be modified. Matra is receiving government funding in this programme, which by early 1982 had completed initial studies with Aérospatiale which had led to the design of neat twin launchers based on a light-alloy rail housing electronic circuits and a purpose-designed circuit for refrigerating the IR homing head of each round. The missile has a pencil-like nose of flat glass panels resembling that of Firestreak, within which is the sensitive seeker, electric servomotor driving canard control fins and, further to the rear, the proximity-fuzed warhead. Much effort has gone into perfecting the target acquisition system, which is expected to comprise either a stabilized optical telescope or (at short ranges) a helmet sight, to which the IR seeker is slaved. The main market is expected to be anti-armour helicopters which could mount the twin launcher in clusters. HATCP can be fired with only very brief exposure

out fin-tips give the missile stability, and correct roll and gravity-drop. Several thousand Genies had been built when production ceased in 1962; the improved TU-289 motor remained in production to 1982.

Above: The nuclear-warhead Genie was not supplied for use by the CF-101B interceptors of the Canadian Armed Forces and the only users are the dwindling F-106 ANG squadrons.

of the launch aircraft, and has exceptionally high average flight speed.

Above: SATCP, an infantry SAM, provides the basis for HATCP.

IR-AAM

In 1981 Mitsubishi Heavy Industries of Japan began development and pre-series manufacture of the IR-AAM (self-explanatory) under contract to the Japan Development Agency's Technical R&D Institute. It will be a highly manoeuvrable dogfight missile using experience gained with AAM-1 and AAM-2 described earlier. No details are available.

Magic, R.550

Origin: SA Matra, France.
Propulsion: SNPE Romeo (Magic I) or Richard (Magic II) Butalane high-impulse solid motor.
Dimensions: Length 109in (2770mm); body diameter 6.2in (157mm); span 26.3in (668mm).
Weight: At launch 198lb (89.8kg).
Performance: Speed about Mach 3; range 0.2-6.2 miles (0.32-10km).
Warhead: Conventional rod/fragmentation, 27.6lb (12.5kg) with all-sector proximity fuze or impact-loop detonation.
Users: Total of 15 countries by late 1982; not listed by Matra but including Abu Dhabi, Argentina, Ecuador, Egypt, France, Greece, India, Iraq, Kuwait, Libya, Oman, Pakistan, Saudi Arabia and South Africa.

Alone among European companies Matra took on the Sidewinder in head-on competition and has not merely achieved technical success but has also established 14 export customers and an output rate exceeding that of any other AAM ever produced in Western Europe. Wisely the weapon was made installationally interchangeable with Sidewinder, but the design requirements were greater than those of presently available versions of the US missile, including launch anywhere within a 140° forward hemisphere at all heights up to 59,000ft (18,000m) and with limitations at higher altitudes; ability to engage from almost any target aspect (head-on will shortly be achieved); ability to snap-fire at ranges down to 984ft (300m); ability to fire from a launch platform flying at any speed (no minimum) up to over 808mph (1300km/h) whilst pulling up to 6g; and ability to pull 3.5g and cross in front of the launch aircraft only 164ft (50m) ahead. The IR guidance uses a Meteor of the SAT type AD.3601, the PbS seeker being cooled prior to launch by a liquid-nitrogen bottle in the launch rail. Its output drives the electric control section with four canard fins (almost the reverse shape of those of Super 530) stationed immediately downstream of four fixed fins with the same span as the tips of the controls. The tail fins are free to rotate around the nozzle. Propulsion is by an SNPE Roméo single-stage composite-DB motor which gives high acceleration for 1.9sec. The warhead weighs 27.6lb (12.5kg) of which half is the explosive charge detonated by IR proximity and DA fuzes. Matra began development as a company venture in 1968, receiving an Air Ministry contract in 1969. After various simpler air trials a missile with guidance was fired from a Meteor of the CEL against a CT-20 target in a tight turn on 11 January 1972. On 30 November 1973 a Magic was fired from a Mirage III in an extreme test of manoeuvrability. IOC was reached in 1975, since when production at Salbris has built up to the rate of 100 per month. Unit price is in the order of $15,000, and more than 6,000 rounds have been delivered.

Right: Demonstration flight by a prototype Mirage 2000 with eight bombs, two tanks, and two short-range Magics.

Below: Manufacturer's cutaway of R.550 Magic showing the disposition of main elements. The umbilical feeds liquid nitrogen to cool the seeker.

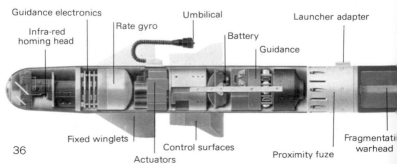

Guidance electronics
Infra-red homing head
Rate gyro
Umbilical
Battery
Guidance
Launcher adapter
Fixed winglets
Control surfaces
Actuators
Proximity fuze
Fragmentati warhead

Above: Magic mounted on the wingtip launcher of a Mirage F1.C of the Armée de l'Air. Safety-pin flags are in English and French.

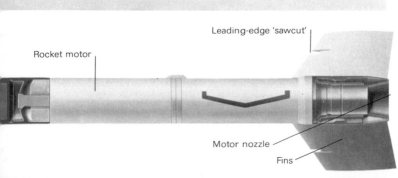

Leading-edge 'sawcut'

Rocket motor

Motor nozzle

Fins

Mica

Origin: SA Matra, France.
Data: Not yet available.

Mica (Missile intermédiat de combat aérien) is a French government funded development with the objective of stretching the Magic airframe to accommodate a longer-burning motor to achieve so-called intermediate range (but not in the same class as Amraam). It may have a choice of guidance methods because according to unofficial reports one version will have a Thomson-CSF active radar. This may be the last generation of air-launched missiles developed in France in preference to a collaborative programme.

MLMS (Air-Launched Stinger)

Origin: General Dynamics Pomona Division, USA.
Propulsion: Tandem Atlantic Research solid motors, high-thrust launch motor and longer-burn flight motor.
Dimensions: Length 60in (1524mm); body diameter 2.75in (69.85mm); span (fins extended) 3.6in (91.4mm).
Weight: At launch 22.3lb (10.1kg); with launcher 34.5lb (15.6kg); complete twin launch installation with electronics and cooling system 99lb (45kg).
Performance: Speed, supersonic; range up to 3 miles (4.8km).
Warhead: Picatinny Arsenal fragmentation, 6.6lb (3kg).
Users: US Army initially.

From the well-known Stinger infantry SAM, GD Pomona is developing a range of other weapons, including the MLMS (multipurpose lightweight missile system) and also ADSM (p.66). MLMS uses either the standard Stinger, as now widely used by US troops, or the much more effective Stinger-POST (passive optical seeker technique) which replaces the simple IR homing by an advanced two-colour (IR and UV) guidance using the latest IRCCM logic circuits and with a unique rosette scan which significantly enhances target detection. MLMS is intended for all battlefield helicopters, and since early 1982 studies have also included the A-10A and Alpha Jet fixed-wing aircraft. A fire-and-forget weapon, Stinger is issued as a certified round in its sealed launch tube and requires no attention between delivery and launch. The basic launcher houses the seeker coolant reservoir and modular electronics and can be stacked three or four deep, giving a total of 16 rounds. For high-speed aircraft a faired launcher is available, enclosing the twin missile tubes. The pilot has a reticle sight or HUD, control panel and a select/uncage/fire control on his cyclic stick, launch

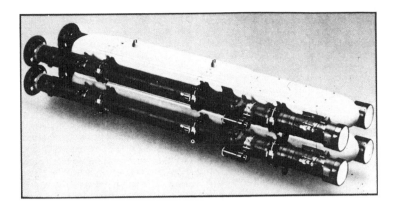

being made when the acquisition tone is heard in his headset. Originally a company initiative, MLMS received DoD funding from 1981; nevertheless, despite the clear (indeed urgent) need for MLMS, and interest from many quarters, the US Army had failed to approve the ROC (required operational capability) by October 1982.

Above: Mock-up of the quad launcher for MLMS, which itself houses the system electronic cards and seeker refrigeration.

Below: Mock-up of twin launch installation on a Westland Lynx 3, which also has a quad group of anti-tank Hellfires.

Phoenix

Origin: Hughes Aircraft, USA.
Propulsion: Aerojet (ATSC) Mk 60 or Rocketdyne Flexadyne Mk 47 long-burn solid motors.
Dimensions: Length 157.8in (4.01m); body diameter 15in (380mm); span 36.4in (925mm).
Weight: 985lb (447kg).
Performance: Speed Mach 5-plus; range over 124 miles (200km).
Warhead: Continuous-rod (132lb, 60kg) with proximity and impact fuzes.
Users: USA (Navy); Iran (484 supplied, remainder possibly in storage).

By far the most sophisticated and costly AAM in the world, this missile provides air defence over an area exceeding 12,000 square miles (31,000km²) from near sea level to the limits of altitude attained by aircraft or tactical missiles. But it can be fired only from the F-14 Tomcat and costs nearly half a million dollars.

Following the classic aerodynamics of the Falcon family, Phoenix was originally AAM-N-11 and Hughes Aircraft began development in 1960 to replace the AIM-47A and Eagle as partner to the AWG-9 for the F-111B. This advanced fire-control system was the most capable ever attempted, and includes a very advanced radar (derived from the ASG-18 carried in the YF-12A) of high-power PD type with the largest circular aerial (of planar type) ever carried by a fighter. It has look-down capability out to ranges exceeding 150 miles (241km), and is backed up by an IR tracker to assist positive target identification and discrimination. AWG-9 has TWS capability, and an F-111B with the maximum load of six Phoenix missiles could engage and attack six aircraft at maximum range simultaneously, weather conditions and target aspect being of little consequence; indeed the basic interception mode assumed is head-on, which is one of the most difficult at extreme range.

Propulsion is by a long-burning Rocketdyne (Flexadyne) Mk 47 or Aerojet Mk60 motor, giving a speed to burnout of Mach 3.8. Combined with low induced drag and the power of the large hydraulically driven tail controls this gives sustained manoeuvrability over a range not even approached by any other AAM, despite the large load of electrical battery, electrical conversion unit, autopilot, electronics unit, transmitter/receiver and planar-array seeker head (all part of the DSQ-26 on-board guidance) as well as the 132lb (60kg) annular blast fragmentation warhead with Downey Mk 334 proximity fuze, Bendix IR fuze and DA fuze.

Hughes began flight test at PMTC in 1965, using a DA-3B Skywarrior, achieving an interception in September 1966. In March 1969 an F-111B successfully engaged two drones, and subsequently Phoenix broke virtually all AAM records including four kills in one pass (out of a six-on-six test, there being one no-test and one miss), a kill on a BQM-34A simulating a cruise missile at 50ft (15m), and a kill on a BQM-34E flying at Mach 1.5 tracked from 153 miles (246km), the Phoenix launched at 127 miles (204km) and impacting 83.5 miles (134km) from the launch point. The first AWG-9 system for the F-14A Tomcat, which replaced the F-111B, was delivered in February 1970. Production of Phoenix AIM-54A at Tucson began in 1973, since when output averaged about 40 per month. By the third quarter of 1978 output had passed 2,500; it then slowed sharply and ended in 1980.

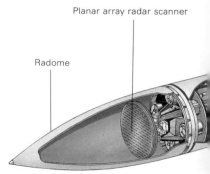

Planar array radar scanner

Radome

Above: Launch of third AIM-54C from PMTC YF-14A No 157990.

Since late 1977 production missiles were of the AIM-54B type with sheet-metal wings and fins instead of honeycomb structure, non-liquid hydraulic and thermal-conditioning systems, and simplified engineering. In 1977 Hughes began a major effort to produce an updated Phoenix to meet the needs of the 1990s. This missile, AIM-54C, has totally new all-digital electronics, more reliable and flexible in use than the analog unit, with a solid-state radar replacing the previous klystron tube model.

Accuracy is improved by a new strapdown inertial reference unit from Nortronics, and ECCM capability is greatly enhanced. Another improvement is a new proximity fuze developed by the Naval Weapons Center. Hughes delivered 15 engineering models from summer 1980, the first firing (head-on against a QF-4, the missile being in the semi-active mode throughout) being successful on 2 June 1980. Then followed 30 pilot-production rounds in the second half of 1981, with full production following from mid-1982. There is a possibility AIM-54A missiles may be updated.

Below: This cutaway shows AIM-54A; AIM-54C differs only in the miniaturized digital avionic section and radar. Phoenix is the only active-radar AAM in the West.

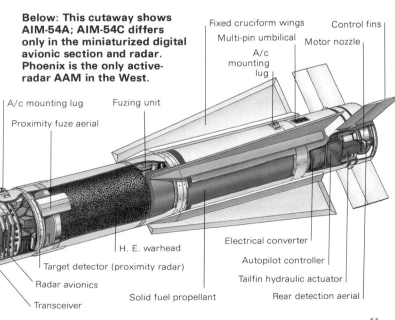

Fixed cruciform wings

Multi-pin umbilical

Control fins

A/c mounting lug

Motor nozzle

A/c mounting lug

Fuzing unit

Proximity fuze aerial

H. E. warhead

Electrical converter

Target detector (proximity radar)

Autopilot controller

Radar avionics

Tailfin hydraulic actuator

Solid fuel propellant

Rear detection aerial

Transceiver

Piranha

Origin: CTA Instituto de Atividades Espaciais, Brazil.
Propulsion: Solid motor.
Dimensions: Length 105in (2.67m); body diameter 6in (152mm); fin span 25.7in (652mm).
Weight: At launch 190lb (86kg).
Performance: Range 3.7 miles (6km).
Warhead: HE 26.5lb (12kg).
User: Brazil.

The Brazilian Air Force has been developing this AAM since 1979. Its homing head has a cooled IR detector, and the autopilot uses proportional navigation applied via canard controls. The warhead has DA and proximity fuzes.

Python 3

Origin: Rafael Armament Development Authority, Israel.
Propulsion: Rafael solid motor.
Dimensions: Not released.
Weight: Not released.
Performance: Claimed superior in speed, turn radius and range to AIM-9L Sidewinder.
Warhead: Conventional rod-type, at least 24lb (11kg).
User: Israel.

First exhibited at the 1981 Paris airshow, this AAM is being developed as a successor to Shafrir II and is claimed to surpass its predecessor in all respects. Rafael is responsible for most parts of Python 3 including

R.530

Origin: SA Matra, France.
Propulsion: Hotchkiss-Brandt/ SNPE Antoinette motor with Plastargol filling (18,740lb, 8500kg, boost for 2.7 sec followed by 6.5 sec sustain) or SNPE Madeleine with Isolane propellant giving higher performance.
Dimensions: Length (radar) 129.3in (3284mm), (IR) 125.9in (3198mm); body diameter 10.35in (263mm); span 43.43in (1103mm).
Weight: At launch, (radar) 423.3lb (192kg), (IR) 426.6lb (193.5kg).
Performance: Speed Mach 2.7; range 11 miles (18km).
Warhead: Hotchkiss-Brandt, two types each of 60lb (27kg), either pre-fragmented or continuous rod; both proximity and DA fuzed.
Users: Argentina, Australia, Brazil, Colombia, France, Iraq, Israel, Lebanon, Pakistan, South Africa, Spain, Venezuela. (Many no longer active).

By 1957 Matra had become the most experienced AAM company in Europe, and work began on this completely new weapon which has ▶

Right: A frame from a high-speed ciné film showing an R.530 being launched from an underwing pylon of a Mirage F1.C.

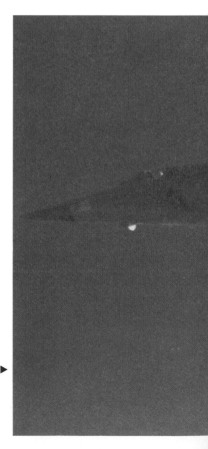

Above: This gaily painted Python 3 shows the way in which the four slipstream-driven rollerons are freely pivoted to the four fixed tailfins. Their gyroscopic effect prevents the missile from rolling, thus easing guidance problems.

the new IR seeker cell (housed in a slightly tapering forebody), which is claimed to have exceptional sensitivity and a wider look-angle than that of most other IR-homing missiles. The delta canard controls are large, as are the fixed tailfins which are sharply swept on both leading and trailing edges, and which carry roll-control aerodynamic surfaces and slipstream-driven rollerons. Deliveries for service use are expected in 1983-4.

enjoyed a long and successful life. Abandoning twist-and-steer, the company reverted to cruciform delta wings and tail controls, two of the wings having ailerons for roll control. Having experience of various guidance systems, the Air Ministry and Matra still could not make up their minds and at first conducted trial firings with either SARH or IR homing. Both types became established in production and to this day R.530 is normally carried in pairs, one missile being a heat-homer and the other a radar-homer.

Propulsion is by a dual-thrust solid motor. The two homing heads, which can if necessary be exchanged by a user squadron to suit circumstances on operations, are the SAT type AD.3501 IR seeker, claimed to have all-aspect capability including head-on, and the EMD type AD.26 matched to the Cyrano Ibis or II of Mirage III interceptors or the Cyrano IV of the Mirage F1. A slightly different receiver is used by the Aéronavale for missiles carried by the F-8E(FN) Crusader, with APQ-94 radar.

Though an indifferent performer, with an unimpressive record of firing trials, R.530 had no evident rival and cleaned up a 14-nation market with some 4,400 rounds sold, at a typical price of $44,000.

Super 530

Origin: SA Matra, France.
Propulsion: SNPE Angèle Butalane high-impulse (composite CTPB) solid motor, 2-sec boost and 4-sec sustain.
Dimensions: Length 139.4in (3.54m); body diameter 10.35in (263mm); span (wing) 25.2in (640mm), (tail) 35.43in (900mm).
Weight: At launch 551lb (250kg); early production 529lb (240kg).
Performance: Speed Mach 4.6; range (early production) 22 miles (35km), (530F) "several dozen km".
Warhead: Thomson-Brandt fragmentation, over 66lb (30kg).
Users: Not announced but export orders from 10 countries.

By January 1971, when development of this missile started, Matra was a mature AAM producer able to take a studied look at the requirements and secure in the knowledge that R.530 would probably remain in production almost a further decade. Though to a slight degree based on the R.530, as reflected in the designation, this is in fact a totally new missile marking very large advances in flight performance and offering doubled acquisition distance and effective range and also introducing snap-up capability of 25,000ft (7600m), since increased to 29,500ft (9000m), believed to exceed that of any other AAM other than Phoenix. From the start only one method of guidance has been associated with Super 530, SARH. This uses the EMD Super AD-26, matched with the Cyrano IV radar of the Mirage F1. Electric power comes from a silver/zinc battery with 60-sec operation. Thomson-Brandt developed the Angèle propulsion motor, with Butalane

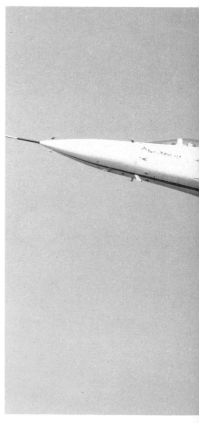

Above: This picture of R.530 on the centreline rack of an early Mirage IIIC was taken in the early 1960s. This Mirage has no SEP.844 booster rocket.

Below: Two Super 530 missiles carried by the second prototype Mirage 2000. The contrast with the R.530 is as great as between the 2000 and the IIIC.

Above: An early Super 530 test firing from a Mirage F1.C trials prototype. The earliest tests were undertaken from Mirages and a Canberra of the CEV at Cazaux in 1974 (inset, Super 530 on Canberra wing pylon). Today the Super 530 is the standard medium-range AAM of the Armée de l'Air Mirage F1.C squadrons. The first Super 530s were received by EC12 (the 12th fighter wing) at Cambrai in December 1979, and soon confirmed its ability to accelerate rapidly to Mach 3 and climb or dive to hit targets 10km (33,000ft) higher or lower than the launch aircraft.

Right: Super 530s and Magics carried by an F1.C of EC.12. For some time Matra has been working on ways of improving this radar-homing weapon.

▶ composite propellant of much higher specific impulse than that of earlier French motors. This can accelerate the missile rapidly to Mach 4.6, thereafter sustaining approximately this speed to sustainer burnout. Wings are not necessary at this speed, but Super 530 does have four wings of very low aspect ratio, manoeuvring by the cruciform of tail fins which have an unusual shape. It can pull 20g up to 56,000ft (17km) and 6g at 82,000ft (25km). The homing head was test-flown in September 1972, and an inert missile airframe was air-launched in July 1973. Firing trials from a Canberra of the CEV began in 1974, progressing to trials with guidance in 1975. Firing trials from a Mirage F1.C began at Cazaux in 1976, and evaluation firing at CEAM has been in progress since 1975, targets in 1978 including the supersonic Beech AQM-37A for which Matra has concluded a licensing/marketing agreement. Super 530F, the version for the Mirage F1, entered service in December 1979, and more than 2,000 rounds had been delivered by mid-1982. In 1984 production will begin on the Super 530D (D for doppler) matched to the RDI radar of the Mirage 2000. This version will have good snap-down performance.

RBS 70

Origin: Saab Bofors Missile Corporation, Sweden.
Propulsion: Bofors solid boost motor; IMI (UK) solid sustainer.
Dimensions: Length 52in (1.32m); body diameter 4.17in (106mm); span (fins extended) 12.6in (320mm).
Weight: At launch (bare missile) 33lb (15kg); (with launch tube) 48.5lb (22kg).
Performance: Speed, supersonic; range 3 miles (5km).
Warhead: Pre-fragmented, 2.2lb (1kg), with optical proximity and DA fuzes.
User: Not yet available.

RBS 70 was produced by AB Bofors (then, in 1974-78, not associated with Saab) as a SAM for use by infantry, with several significant advantages over earlier man-portable weapons in this class. The missile is popped out of its tube by a short-burn motor which drops off just beyond the mouth of the tube. Fins and midposition wings unfold and the sustainer then accelerates the round to well beyond Mach 1. Guidance is by riding a laser beam held on the target; any deviation from the beam is sensed and processed by an on-board computer which sends signals to the control fins. By 1980 RBS 70, whose development was part-funded by Switzerland, was in the hands of troops in Sweden and Switzerland and Saab-Bofors was studying other versions. At the 1981 Paris airshow a portion of Lynx helicopter was exhibited carrying on a left-side pylon a four-round launcher (another would be mounted on the right side) for an AAM version. The system would include a Saab Helios roof-mounted

Red Top

Origin: Hawker Siddeley (now British Aerospace) Dynamics, UK.
Propulsion: Single-stage solid motor.
Dimensions: Length 130.6in (3.32m); body diameter 8.75in (222.25mm); span 35.75in (908mm).
Weight: At launch 330lb (150kg).
Performance: Speed at burnout Mach 3.2; range up to 7.5 miles (12km).
Warhead: Conventional fragmentation, 68.3lb (31kg).
Users: Saudi Arabia, UK (RAF).

Originally called Firestreak Mk IV, this was a rationalised Firestreak with the components reassembled in a more logical arrangement, and with a completely new seeker head, motor and warhead to give very much greater lethality. The basic requirement, of late 1956, was to produce a missile not confined to the ± 15° squint angle of first-generation IR seekers, and, by developing a seeker able to home on the target's jet itself, or other hot parts, attack successfully from any direction. As early as 1958 an American publication reported that "Red Top. . .has a 68lb conventional warhead and a range of 14,000 yards, with. . .a cooled lead telluride cell receiving in a 4 to 5 micro range". Though slightly garbled, this disclosed valuable information which at the time was highly classified, and even today no details of the seeker may be given. In the course of development the missile was redesigned with an untapered forebody to accommodate a larger warhead. The improved

sight with auto-handover after launch of the chosen round(s). With the helicopter hull-down, only the sight being visible to the enemy, the control unit boresights the video tracker to the target aircraft so that the laser can designate the target through

Above: RBS 70 quad installation for trials on Lynx AH.1.

the same optical window. Alternatively, target designation can be from a remote friendly laser, the helicopter remaining passive.

motor gave a speed of just over Mach 3 at burnout, while the nose was redesigned as a full-diameter glass hemisphere. Wings and tail controls were completely redesigned with greater area, and with planform and section profile matched to Mach 3, greater altitudes and much greater lateral acceleration. The powerful warhead, of a new type, had a later IR fuzing system in advance of any other AAM system of the late 1950s. It was positioned as a single package ahead of the wings, while the control group was relocated next to the control fins. Development was rapid and successful, and by late 1964 a

few Red Tops were being issued to 74 Sqn, whose Lightnings were being upgraded to F.3 (later F.6) standard with a larger vertical tail to counter the slightly larger side area of the new missile. At the same time Red Top was issued to the first RN squadron equipped with the Sea Vixen FAW.2, No 899, replacing Firestreak on four wing pylons. Red Top was subsequently improved in small details and remains in service with Lightnings of the RAF, and Saudi Arabia (mostly in storage).

Below: Red Tops on unpainted Lightning F.6 of RAF No 23 Sqn.

SA-7

Origin: Soviet Union.
Propulsion: Dual-thrust boost/sustain solid motor.
Dimensions: Length 53.25in (1350mm); body diameter 2.75in (70mm); fin span 7.9in (200mm).
Weight: At launch, 20.3lb (9.2kg).
Performance: Speed Mach 1.5;

range 0.5-3 miles (0.8-5km).
Warhead: Conventional fragmentation, 5.5lb (2.5kg), graze and DA fuzes.
Users: In AAM role, believed only Soviet Union.

Called Grail by NATO, the SA-7 was

Shafrir

Origin: Rafael Armament Development Authority, Israel.
Propulsion: Solid motor.
Dimensions: Length 97in (2470mm); body diameter 6.3in (160mm); span 20.5in (520mm).
Weight: At launch (Mk 2) 205lb (93kg).
Performance: Speed supersonic; range 3.1 miles (5km).
Warhead: Conventional 24.3lb (11kg) containing 8.8lb (4kg) explosive plus pre-fragmented bodies, with row of IR fuze windows around nose and also DA fuze.
Users: Chile, Israel, South Africa and Taiwan and from four to ten other (undisclosed) countries.

Development of this wholly Israeli AAM, derived by Rafael Armament Development Authority from early Sidewinders, was started in 1961, and by 1965 Shafrir had in many respects overtaken the US missile. Many details are still classified but it is clear that all models have a Cassegrain optical system behind a large hemispherical nose, pneumatic control fins, and fixed wings indexed in line and containing recessed rollerons similar to those of Sidewinder. The most fundamental difference introduced with the Israeli weapon is a substantial increase in body diameter, which must greatly improve many aspects of design and lethality. Simplicity was the keynote throughout, and a price of $20,000 has been quoted. Mk 1 did not complete development, but Mk 2 entered Chel Ha'Avir service in 1969, and in subsequent fighting is credited with the destruction of over 200 aircraft. Of these more than half were destroyed during the brief Yom Kippur war in October 1973, claimed to indicate an SSKP of 60 per cent. Mk

Below: Drawn for this book, this cutaway shows the disposition of major elements in Shafrir 2. The pneumatically-driven canards pivot in pairs, as seen in the photograph above.

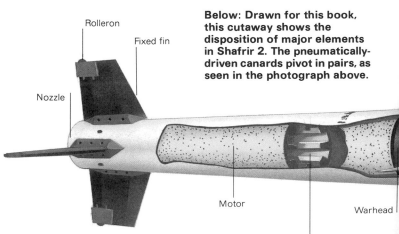

Rolleron
Fixed fin
Nozzle
Motor
Warhead
Cross-section of propellant

originally a SAM for use by infantry. A rudimentary weapon, it has IR homing which cannot be relied upon to achieve lock-on to an approaching aircraft, though the seeker has been progressively improved. Over 50,000 rounds have been exported to at least 22 countries, and it is a favoured terrorist weapon. As in other countries the Soviet Union has used this SAM as a self-defence weapon for helicopters, twin and four-barrel pods having been seen since 1981 mounted on various types of Mi-24 (Hind). No details are yet available of the way targets are acquired, but anti-armour Mi-24 versions are well equipped with sighting and weapon cueing systems. The seeker of land-based SA-7 missiles is uncooled, so aircraft installation problems should be minimal.

2 is carried on a pylon adapter, which can also carry alternative weapons. When the seeker locks-on, the pilot is informed both visually and aurally. The Mk 2 homes by lead-collision using proportional navigation. This model is used by the Chel Ha'Avir on Mirages and Kfirs, and also by several export customers.

Above: Compared with Sidewinder, Shafrir has a body of larger diameter (160 against 127mm). This is on a Kfir pylon.

Mk 3 has been under test for several years and has a later guidance and control section; it has been renamed Python 3 (see p.42).

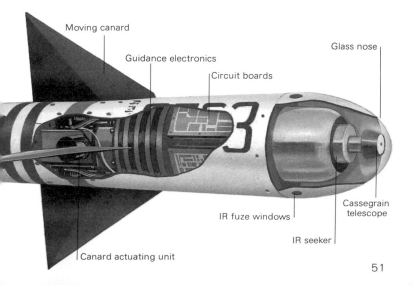

Moving canard

Guidance electronics

Circuit boards

Glass nose

Cassegrain telescope

IR fuze windows

IR seeker

Canard actuating unit

Sidewinder, AIM-9

Origin: Original design by US Naval Weapons Center, China Lake; commercial production by Philco (now Ford Aerospace) and later GE, today shared by Ford Aerospace (most versions, currently 9L and 9P) and Raytheon (9L and 9M).

Propulsion: Solid motor (various, by Rockwell, Aerojet or Thiokol, with Aerojet Mk 17 qualified on 9B/E/J/N/P and Thiokol Mk 36 or reduced-smoke TX-683 qualified on 9L/M).

Dimensions: See variants table.

Weight: See variants table.

Performance: See variants table.

Warhead: (B/E/J/N/P) 10lb (4.5kg) blast/fragmentation with passive IR proximity fuze (from 1982 being refitted with Hughes DSU-21/B active laser fuze), (D/G/H) 22.4lb (10.2kg) continuous rod with IR or HF proximity fuze, (L/M) 25lb (11.4kg) advanced annular blast/fragmentation with active laser IR proximity fuze.

Users: (all versions) Argentina, Australia, Belgium, Brazil, Canada, Chile, Denmark, West Germany, Greece, Iran, Israel, Italy, Japan, South Korea, Kuwait, Malaysia, Morocco, Netherlands, Norway, Pakistan, Philippines, Portugal, Saudi Arabia, Singapore, Spain, Sweden, Taiwan, Tunisia, Turkey, UK (RAF, RN), USA (all services).

One of the most influential missiles in history, this slim AAM was almost un-American in development for it was created out of nothing by a very small team at NOTS China Lake, operating on the proverbial shoestring budget. Led by Doctor McLean, this team was the first in the world to attack the problem of passive IR homing guidance, in 1949, and the often intractable difficulties were compounded by the choice of an airframe of only 5in (127mm) diameter, which in the days of vacuum-tube electronics was a major challenge. In 1951 Philco was awarded a contract for a homing head based on the NOTS research and today, 28 years later, the guidance team at Newport Beach, now called Ford Aerospace and Communications, is still in production with homing heads for later Sidewinders. The first XAAM-N-7 guided round was successfully fired on 11 September 1953. The first production missiles, called N-7 by the Navy, GAR-8 by the USAF and SW-1 by the development team, reached IOC in May 1956.

These early Sidewinders were made of sections of aluminium tube, with the seeker head and control fins at the front and four fixed tail fins containing patented rollerons at the back. The rolleron is similar to

Below: Live AIM-9M (improved 9L) Sidewinders need careful handling and a powered loader is being used here.

an air-driven gyro wheel, and one is mounted in the tip of each fin so that it is spun at high speed by the slipstream. The original solid motor was made by Hunter-Douglas, Hercules and Norris-Thermador, to Naval Propellant Plant design, and it accelerated the missile to Mach 2.5 in 2.2 sec.

The beauty of this missile was its simplicity, which meant low cost, easy compatibility with many aircraft and, in theory, high reliability in harsh environments. It was said to have "less than 24 moving parts" and "fewer electronic components than the average radio". At the same time, though the guidance method meant that Sidewinder could be carried by any fighter, with or without radar, it was erratic in use and restricted to close stern engagements at high altitude in good visibility. The uncooled PbS seeker gave an SSKP of about 70 per cent in ideal conditions, but extremely poor results in bad visibility, cloud or rain, or at low levels, and showed a tendency to lock-on to the Sun, or bright sky, or reflections from lakes or rivers.

The pilot energised his missile homing head and listened for its ▶

Sidewinder Guidance Sections

	AIM-9B: 80,900 produced by Philco and GE and c15,000 by European consortium; 10,000+ updated by Ford.
	AIM-9C/D: 9C SARH model by Motorola (1,000+), 9D with better IR/speed/manoeuvre, 950+ by Ford for US Navy.
	AIM-9E: 9B rebuilt with new cooled wide-angle seeker, about 5,000 for USAF by Ford (Aeronutronic).
	AIM-9G/H: 9G improved 9D with off-boresight lock-on (2,120 Raytheon, USN); 9H solid-state (3,000 Ford AF).
	AIM-9L/M: 9L 3rd generation all-aspect (Ford and Raytheon, also Europe); 9M improved ECCM/motor (Raytheon).
	AIM-9J/N: J rebuilt B/E with new front end (Ford c14,000 for AF); N (formerly J1) further improved (c,7,000).
	AIM-9P improved B/E/J or new production, new motor/fuze and better reliability, c13,000 by Ford for USAF.

signals in his headset. It would give a growl when it acquired a target, and if it was nicely positioned astern of a hot jetpipe the growl would become a fierce strident singing that would rise in intensity until the pilot let the missile go. There were plenty of QF-80, Firebee and other targets that had early Sidewinders up their jetpipe in the 1950s, but unfortunately real-life engagements tended to have the wrong target, or the wrong aspect, or the wrong IR-emitting background. In October 1958, however, large numbers of Sidewinders were fired by Nationalist Chinese F-86s against Chinese MiG-17s and 14 of the latter were claimed in one day. This was the first wartime use of AAMs.

The staggering total of nearly 81,000 of the original missile were built in three almost identical versions which in the new 1962 scheme were designated AIM-9, 9A and 9B. Nearly all were of the 9B form, roughly half produced by Philco (Ford) and half by Raytheon. A further 15,000 were delivered by a European consortium headed by BGT, which in the late 1960s gave each European missile a new seeker head of BGT design known as FGW Mod 2. This has a nose dome of silicon instead of glass, a cooled seeker and semi-conductor electronics, and transformed the missile's reliability and ability to lock-on in adverse conditions.

By 1962 SW-1C was in use in two versions, AIM-9C by Motorola and -9D by Ford. This series introduced the Rocketdyne Mk 36 solid motor giving much greater range, a new airframe with tapered nose, long-chord controls and more swept leading edges on the tail fins, and completely new guidance. Motorola produced the 9C for the F-8 Crusader, giving it SARH guidance matched to the Magnavox APQ-94 radar, but for various reasons this odd man out was unreliable in performance and was withdrawn. In contrast, 9D was so successful it formed the basis of many subsequent versions, as well as MIM-72C Chaparral. The new guidance section introduced a dome of magnesium fluoride, a nitrogen-cooled seeker, smaller field of view, and increased reticle speed and tracking speed. The control section introduced larger fins, which

The Sidewinder Family

Model	Guidance	Length
AIM-9B	Uncooled PbS. 25° look. 70 Hz reticle. 11°/sec tracking	111.4in (2830mm)
9B FGW.2	CO_2 cooling, solar dead zone reduced to 5°	114.5in (2908mm)
AIM-9C	Motorola SARH	113.0in (2870mm)
AIM-9D	N_2 cooled PbS, 40° look, 125 Hz reticle, 12°/sec tracking	113.0in (2870mm)
AIM-9E	Peltier-cooled PbS, 40° look, 100 Hz reticle, 16.5°/sec tracking	118.1in (3000mm)
AIM-9G	As -9D plus SEAM	113.0in (2870mm)
AIM-9H	As -9G plus solid-state, 20°/sec tracking	113.0in (2870mm)
AIM-9J	As -9E plus part-solid-state	120.9in (3070mm)
AIM-9L	Argon-cooled InSb. fixed reticle, tilted mirror system	112.2in (2850mm)
AIM-9M	As -9L, better motor and ECCM	112.2in (2850mm)
AIM-9N	As -9E plus part-solid-state	120.9in (3070mm)
AIM-9P	As -9N plus reliability improvements	120.9in (3070mm)

Above: Early production F-16A with two 9L (tips), two 9J, two Mk 84 (2,000lb) bombs, two tanks and an ALQ-119 ECM pod.

were detachable, and high-power actuators fed by a longer-burning gas generator. The old 10lb (4.54kg) warhead with passive-IR fuze was replaced by a 22.4lb (10.2kg) annular blast fragmentation head of the continuous-rod type, fired by either an IR or HF proximity fuze.

AIM-9E was fitted with a greatly improved Ford seeker head with Peltier (thermoelectric) cooling, further-increased tracking speed and new electronics and wiring harnesses, giving increased engagement boundaries especially at low level. AIM-9G has so-called SEAM. (Sidewinder Expanded Acquisition Mode), an improved 9D seeker head, but was overtaken by 9H. The latter introduced solid-state electronics, even faster tracking speed, and double-delta controls with increased actuator power, giving greater manoeuvrability than any previous Sidewinder as well as limited all-weather capability. AIM-9J is a rebuilt 9B or 9E

with part-solid-state electronics, detachable double-delta controls with greater power, and long-burning gas generator. Range is sacrificed for high acceleration to catch fast targets.

There are J-1 and J-3 improved or "all-new" variants. A major advance came with Sidewinder 9L, with which NWC (as NOTS now is) at last responded to the prolonged demands of customers and the proven accomplishments of BGT. The latter's outstanding seeker head developed for Viper was first fitted to AIM-9L to give Alasca (All-Aspect Capability), a great missile that was merely used by Germany as a possible fall-back in case 9L failed to mature. AIM-9L itself, in full production from 1977, has long-span pointed delta fins, a totally new guidance system (see table), and an annular blast fragmentation warhead sheathed in a skin of preformed rods, triggered by a new proximity fuze in which a ring of eight GaAs laser diodes emit and a ring of silicon photodiodes receive.

About 16,000 of the 9L series were expected to be made by 1983, and at least a further 9,000 are likely to be made by a new BGT-led European consortium which this time includes BAe Dynamics and companies in Norway and Italy. Pilot production deliveries began in 1981, and BAe received its first production contract (for £40 million) in February 1982. No European missiles had reached British squadrons in April 1982 and 100 AIM-9L were supplied for use by Harriers and Sea Harriers in the South Atlantic from US stocks, gaining 25 known victories.

AIM-9M is a revised L. 9N is the new designation of J-1 (all are 9B or 9E rebuilds). 9P are rebuilds of 9B/E/J, and additional 9P missiles are being made from new.

Control fin span	Launch wt	Mission time	Range	Production
22.0in (559mm)	155lb (70.4kg)	20 sec	2 miles (3.2 km)	80,900
22.0in (559mm)	167lb (75.8kg)	20 sec	2.3 miles (3.7 km)	15,000
24.8in (630mm)	185lb (84.0kg)	60 sec	11 miles (17.7 km)	1,000
24.8in (630mm)	195lb (88.5kg)	60 sec	11 miles (17.7 km)	1,000
22.0in (559mm)	164lb (74.5kg)	20 sec	2.6 miles (4.2 km)	5,000 (ex-9B)
24.8in (630mm)	191lb (86.6kg)	60 sec	11 miles (17.7 km)	2,120
24.8in (630mm)	186lb (84.5kg)	60 sec	11 miles (17.7 km)	7,720
22.0in (559mm)	172lb (78.0kg)	40 sec	9 miles (14.5 km)	10,000 (ex-9B)
24.8in (630mm)	188lb (85.3kg)	60 sec	11 miles (17.7 km)	11,700+
24.8in (630mm)	190lb (86.0kg)	60 sec	11 miles (17.7 km)	3,500+
22.0in (559mm)	172lb (78.0kg)	40 sec	9 miles (14.5 km)	7,000
22.0in (559mm)	172lb (78.0kg)	60 sec	11 miles (17.7 km)	13,000

Sky Flash

Origin: British Aerospace Dynamics, UK.

Propulsion: Aerojet or Rockwell Mk 52 PB/AP solid motor.

Dimensions: Length 145in (3680mm); body diameter 8in (203mm); span 40in (1020mm).

Weight: At launch 425lb (193kg).

Performance: Speed Mach 4; range 31 miles (50km).

Warhead: Sparrow-7E type 66lb (30kg) continuous-rod pattern, with proximity and DA fuzes.

Users: Sweden, UK (RAF, possibly RN later).

While the US industry develops its own monopulse seeker for Sparrow, the UK industry began such work in 1969, leading to a brilliant series of test firings in November 1975 and production delivery to the RAF by BAe Dynamics in 1978. Originally XJ.521, and later named Sky Flash, this missile is a 7E2 with a completely new MSDS homing head operating in I-band with inverse processing by all-solid-state microelectronics. The warm-up time has been reduced from about 15 sec to less than 2 sec. The short range of the basic 7E2 is considered acceptable for European conditions, though the 7F motor could be fitted if needed. The trials programme from Point Mugu is judged the most successful of any AAM in history; more than half actually struck the target, often in extremely difficult conditions of glint or evasive manoeuvres, while the miss-distance of the remainder averaged "about one-tenth that of most radar-guided AAMs". Moreover, the warhead is triggered by a deadly EMI active-radar fuze placed behind the seeker, the warhead being behind the wings. Sweden has adopted Sky Flash as RB 71 for the JA 37 Viggen. Sky Flash is carried by RAF Phantoms in the interception role and is matched with Foxhunter radar on the Tornado F.2 interceptor. Sky Flash Mk 2 was unfortunately abandoned by the British government at an advanced stage in early 1981, neatly destroying work which had put the BAe/MSDS team ahead of the world. Instead the American AMRAAM will be purchased.

Below: First test firing of a live Sky Flash, from an F-4J Phantom II of the US Navy at Point Mugu in November 1975. Though everything possible was done to confuse the missiles on test the trials programme went brilliantly.

Above: Two RB 71 Sky Flash AAMs can be seen on this unpainted prototype Saab JA 37 Viggen, as well as two RB 24 Sidewinder close-range missiles. The Swedish government has placed two major Sky Flash contracts.

Below: To accommodate two pairs of Sky Flash missiles nose-to-tail the fuselage of the ADV Tornado interceptor was lengthened by 4ft (1.2m), which in turn enabled internal fuel capacity to be increased for 4½-hour patrol missions.

Sparrow, AIM-7

Origin: (AIM-7E, 7F, 7M) Raytheon Company, USA, with second-source production (7F, M) by GD Pomona and licence-manufacture (7F) by Mitsubishi, Japan.

Propulsion: (7E) Aerojet or Rockwell Mk 52 Mod 2 PB/AP solid motor, (7F, M) Hercules or Aerojet Mk 58 high-impulse solid motor.

Dimensions: Length (E, F) 144in (3660mm), (M) 145in (3680mm); body diameter 8in (203mm); span 40in (1020mm).

Weight: At launch (E) 452lb (205kg), (F, M) 503lb (228kg).

Performance: Speed (both) about Mach 4; range (E) 28 miles (44km). (F, M) 62 miles (100km).

Warhead: (E) 66lb (30kg) continuous-rod warhead, (F, M) 88lb (40kg) Mk 71 advanced continuous-rod warhead, in each case with proximity and DA fuzes.

Users: (AAM use only) West Germany, Greece, Iran, Israel, Italy, Japan, South Korea, Spain, Turkey, UK (RAF), USA (AF, Navy, Marines).

Considerably larger than other contemporary American AAMs, this missile not only progressed through three fundamentally different families, each with a different prime contractor, but late in life mushroomed into totally new versions for quite new missions as an ASM (Shrike, p.134) and a SAM (two types of Sea Sparrow).

Sperry Gyroscope began the programme as Project Hot Shot in 1946, under US Navy BuAer contract. By 1951 Sperry had a contract for full engineering development of XAAM-N-2 Sparrow I, and the suffix I was added because by that time there was already a Sparrow II. The first representative guided flight tests took place in 1953. This missile was a beam rider, with flush dipole aerials around the body which picked up the signals from the fighter radar beam (assumed to be locked-on to the target) and drove the cruciform delta wings to keep the missile aligned in the centre of the beam. At the tail were four fixed fins, indexed in line with the wings. Propulsion was by an Aerojet solid motor, and missile assembly took place at the Sperry-Farragut Division which operated a Naval Industrial Reserve plant at Bristol, Tennessee.

IOC was reached in July 1956, and Sparrow I was soon serving in the Atlantic and Pacific Fleets, and with the Marine Corps.

In 1955 Douglas obtained limited funding for Sparrow II, as main armament for the proposed F5D-1 Skylancer. Amazingly, however, the company did not switch to SARH guidance but to fully active radar, and this was tough in a missile of 8in (203mm) diameter, a figure common to all Sparrows. In mid-1956 the Navy decided to terminate Sparrow II, but it was snapped up by the Royal Canadian Air Force as armament for the Arrow supersonic interceptor. After severe difficulties Premier Diefenbaker cancelled Sparrow II on 23 September 1958, and the Arrow itself the following February.

Three years previously Raytheon had begun to work on Sparrow III, taking over the Bristol plant in 1956. Sparrow III uses almost the same airframe as Sparrow II but with SARH guidance. By the mid-1950s Raytheon had become one of the most capable missile companies, ▶

Right: Test firing of an AIM-7F Sparrow AAM from the seventh development prototype F/A-18A Hornet, which carries two on the flanks of the mid-fuselage.

The Sparrow Family

1950 designation	1962	Guidance	Length
AAM-N-2 Sparrow I	AIM-7A	Radar beam riding	140in (3.56m)
AAM-N-3 Sparrow II	AIM-7B	Active radar homing	144in (3.66m)
AAM-N-6 Sparrow III	AIM-7C	SARH CW	144in (3.66m)
AAM-N-6A/AIM-101	AIM-7D	SARH CW	144in (3.66m)
AAM-N-6B	AIM-7E	SARH CW	144in (3.66m)
—	AIM-7F	SARH CW solid-state	144in (3.66m)
—	AIM-7M	SARH CW solid state	145in (3.68m)

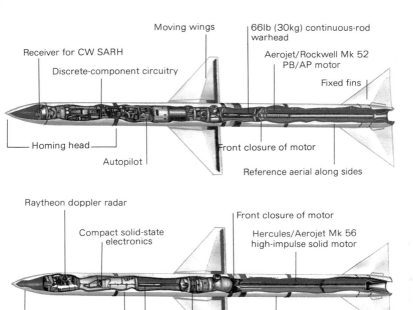

Moving wings

66lb (30kg) continuous-rod warhead

Receiver for CW SARH

Aerojet/Rockwell Mk 52 PB/AP motor

Discrete-component circuitry

Fixed fins

Homing head

Autopilot

Front closure of motor

Reference aerial along sides

Raytheon doppler radar

Front closure of motor

Compact solid-state electronics

Hercules/Aerojet Mk 56 high-impulse solid motor

Improved radome housing conical-scan slotted aerial

Reference aerial

Axial instrumentation funnel

88lb (40kg) Mk 71 continuous-rod warhead

Increased-power hydraulic servo controls

Above: Comparative cutaways of AIM-7E (top) and AIM-7F/7M, showing how in today's Sparrow more compact guidance has enabled the warhead to be moved ahead of the wings, making room for a new motor.

Span	Launch wt	Range	Production
39in (0.99m)	310lb (141kg)	5 miles (8 km)	c2,000
39in (0.99m)	420lb (191kg)	?	c100
40in (1.02m)	380lb (172kg)	25 miles (40 km)	2,000
40in (1.02m)	440lb (200kg)	25 miles (40 km)	7,500
40in (1.02m)	452lb (205kg)	28 miles (44 km)	25,000
40in (1.02m)	503lb (228kg)	62 miles (100 km)	3,000
40in (1.02m)	503lb (228kg)	62 miles (100 km)	1,800+

▶ possibly because its background was electronics rather than airframes. It built up a missile engineering centre at Bedford, Massachusetts, with a test base at Oxnard (not far from Point Mugu), California; production of Sparrows was finally shared between Bristol and a plant at South Lowell, near Bedford.

Most of the airframe is precision-cast light alloy. Early Sparrow III missiles had an Aerojet solid motor, not cast integral with the case, and introduced CW guidance. AIM-7C, as it became, reached IOC in 1958 with Demons of the Atlantic and Pacific fleets. AIM-7D introduced the Thiokol (previously Reaction Motors) prepackaged liquid motor, and was also adopted by the Air Force in 1960 as AIM-101 to arm the F-110 (later F-4C) Phantom. All fighter Phantoms can carry four Sparrows recessed into the underside of the fuselage, with target illumination by the APQ-72, APQ-100, APQ-109, APQ-120, or APG-59 (part of AWG-10 or -11) radar. In the Italian F-104S Starfighter the radar is the Rockwell R-21G/H, and in the F-14 Tomcat the powerful Hughes AWG-9. The AIM-7D was also the basis for PDMS Sea Sparrow.

AIM-7E, the next version (also used in the NATO Sea Sparrow system), uses the Rocketdyne free-standing solid motor with Flexadyne propellant (Mk 38), which gives a slightly increased burnout speed of Mach 3.7. The warhead is of the continuous-rod type, the explosive

SRAAM

Origin: British Aerospace Dynamics, UK.
Propulsion: Advanced solid motor by IMI Summerfield with control actuation (see text) by Sperry Gyroscope (now part of BAe).
Dimensions: 107.25in (2724mm); body diameter 6.5in (165mm).
Weight: Not published.
Performance: Typical of IR-homing dogfight missiles.
Warhead: Not published.
User: Probably R&D only.

Experience in Vietnam rammed home the urgent need for close-range air-combat weapons. HSD (now BAe Dynamics Group) put company money into a study of close-range AAMs. By 1970 the missile, named Taildog, had been completely designed other than details of the solid motor and IR seeker. Later in that year a small MoD contract was received and development proceeded under the name SRAAM (short-range AAM). The contract was terminated in 1974, and replaced by a low-key technology-demonstration programme to be undertaken without urgency and involving merely eight firings, from ground launchers and a Hunter fighter. The first shot with guidance in April 1977 passed within lethal range of a difficult target, triggering the novel BAe fuze. Subsequent firings proved SRAAM's unparalleled manoeuvrability, which can include a 90° turn immediately on leaving the launcher. The objective of the designers, abundantly achieved, was to produce a simple AAM system, of low cost, that could be attached to any aircraft without needing modification of either the aircraft or launcher; to give the pilot unprecedented SSKP in a dogfight, while greatly reducing his workload; and to offer high snap-shot lethality against targets in previously impossible situations such as crossing at minimum range. SRAAM is instantly available and fired automatically as soon as the seeker acquires a target coming into view ahead. It is wingless, and carried in a lightweight twin-tube launcher whose adapter shoe houses the fire-control system. The chosen missile tube flicks open its nose doors, fires the round, and closes the doors to reduce drag. The passive IR seeker commands the missile by motor TVC. In August 1977, when AIM-9L (p.52) was chosen for British use, it was stated that SRAAM would be "kept alive" to provide a coherent design base. An outstandingly successful interception took place on 18 August 1980, using

charge being wrapped in a tight drum made from a continuous rod of stainless steel which shatters into about 2,600 lethal fragments. DA and proximity fuzes are fitted. Many thousands of 7E missiles were used in Vietnam by F-4s, but, owing to the political constraints imposed on the American fighters, were seldom able to be fired. Accordingly AIM-7E2 was developed with shorter minimum range, increased power of manoeuvre and plug-in aerodynamic surfaces requiring no tools. The AIM-7C, D and E accounted for over 34,000 missiles.

Introduced in 1977, AIM-7F has all-solid-state guidance, making room for a more powerful motor, the Hercules Mk 58, giving further-enhanced flight speed and range, as well as a larger (88lb, 40kg) warhead. Claimed to lock-on reasonably well against clutter up to 10 db, -7F is compatible with CW PD radars (and thus with the F-15 and F-18), and has a conical-scan seeker head. In 1977 GD Pomona was brought in as second-source supplier and with Raytheon is expected to deliver about 19,000 missiles by 1985, split roughly equally between the Navy and Air Force, plus hoped-for exports.

In 1982 both contractors switched to AIM-7M, developed by Raytheon. This has an inverse-processed digital monopulse seeker generally similar to Sky Flash in giving greatly improved results in adverse conditions. GD's first contract was for 690, following 3,000 of the 7F type.

Above: BAe SRAAM test missile as seen from trials Hunter.

swivel-nozzle TVC and with four motor-bleed tangential jets for roll control. Much SRAAM knowledge is expected to go into Asraam.

Tirailleur

Dornier GmbH, West Germany, worked on this advanced dogfight missile in 1977-80. Like BAe's SRAAM it featured body lift and in one form motor TVC steering. Both IR and miniature radar guidance were investigated.

V3 Kukri

Origin: Armscor, South Africa.
Propulsion: 2-stage solid motor.
Dimensions: Length 115.75in (2.94m); body diameter 5in (127mm).
Weight: (at launch) 162lb (73kg).
Performance: Speed Mach 2+; range 1000ft-2.5 miles (300-4000m).
Warhead: Fragmentation.

This IR dogfight missile entered production in 1981 to arm SAAF Mirages and Impalas. It has horizontal tandem canard controls and single delta canards in the vertical plane, but no tail rollerons.

Air-to-Surface

ASMs are the most diverse of all classes of missile. The first in this category, in World War 1, were steered by remote control against enemy ships, which were attacked either by the missile's own warhead or by its release of a torpedo. In World War 2 ASMs proliferated in size, warhead, guidance and function, so that by the 1950s the diversity was already astonishing. Some were almost pilotless aeroplanes, laden with thermonuclear warheads that could destroy cities. Few of these are left, though the USAF's cruise missile is at present judged capable of penetrating likely defences and put a nuclear warhead on a particular chosen ICBM (intercontinental ballistic missile) silo. The Soviet Union still has a few large ASMs used in the long-range anti-ship role.

Far more numerous are the sea-skimmers. These are missiles used only against surface ships, and designed to fly just above the ocean surface to make them more difficult to detect and shoot down (and with the extra advantage that their guidance need steer them in one plane only, the up/down plane often being ignored). Most sea skimmers can be fired from ships or submarines as well as from aircraft, and they could have been separated in this book into a chapter of their own were it not for the fact that some also exist in other forms tailored to land targets.

Land targets come in many forms. The largest are cities, which can be targeted by long-range nuclear

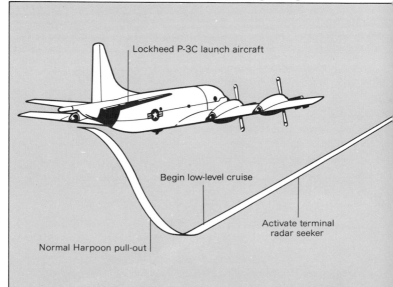

Lockheed P-3C launch aircraft

Begin low-level cruise

Activate terminal radar seeker

Normal Harpoon pull-out

ASMs used in the role of a deterrent to war. Just which of the West's or Warsaw Pact's ASMs are targeted on cities is classified, but this appears to be a task best left to ICBMs and SLBMs (submarine-launched BMs). Cities are neither transient nor mobile and thus form an ideal target for such global-scale weapons. The ASM is almost always used for more difficult targets such as bridges, rail or road junctions, or an army on the march. In the West great effort has also been made to plan ASMs for use against airfields, though airfields are as fixed in position as cities, and form an ideal sitting duck for quite simple nuclear missiles.

The author has never had the slightest doubt that, should the Soviet leaders wish to take over Western Europe, their first move would be to eliminate (totally) NATO airpower with a rain of nuclear missiles on its airfields. NATO planning appears to ignore this, and its own efforts against WP airfields are centred around the difficult task of dropping small bombs and mines on runways, taxi tracks and hardened aircraft shelters. This is quite a challenge even on a fine day with no opposition, and to do it for real is demanding much thought among ASM designers, who are offering such contrasting weapons as Durandal, JP.233 and MRASM.

MRASM, incidentally, is a new version of a cruise missile which in earlier models had a nuclear warhead. If NATO (but not the WP forces) choose to renounce nuclear weapons, as they appear to be doing, they ▶

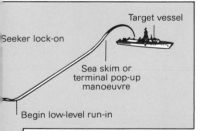

Target vessel

Seeker lock-on

Sea skim or
terminal pop-up
manoeuvre

Begin low-level run-in

Left: The flight profile of the US Navy AGM-84A Harpoon is typical of all air-launched anti-ship missiles. Turbojet propulsion gives long range, enabling the launch aircraft to stay out of SAM range; next-generation ASMs will have supersonic ramjet engines.
Below: Harpoon on P-3C.

►can hardly expect to win. MRASM, if put into service, will have somehow to be carried into the air from an airbase that has been converted into a charred ruin by a nuclear missile. It must then fly several hundred miles, close to the ground and considerably slower than defending fighters, and finally fly with great precision down the centreline of a runway whilst ejecting small bomblets, to cause a row of craters. Does this make sense to a single reader?

In contrast, an army on the march changes in character and position continuously, and fixed targeting is seldom worth while. No modern army is going to offer juicy targets such as an entire armoured division encamped at one place, or even strung along a single road. The defending air force has to maintain constant surveillance, enjoy the best electronic-warfare capability (in all respects, communications, radars, countermeasures, position-fixing, decoys, spoof, IFF, signal intelligence, the lot) that money can buy, and have weapons that can fly by themselves not just on enemy targets but on the selected enemy targets that matter most.

We in the West are a long way from having this capability. Most of our weapons are plain 'iron bombs' and unguided rockets. A few are ASMs with some form of command steering. A much smaller number have automatic homing on to target IR, while if the target can be illuminated by a friendly

Below: Maverick has been produced in more versions and greater quantity than any other tactical ASM. Here an early test AGM-65A with sustainer burning impacts an obsolete AFV target.

laser (aimed by a defending soldier or aircraft) it can attract a so-called smart bomb which flies down to the source of the light diffused away from the target. But future battlefields are no place for aircraft. ASM designers have for years tried to create fire-and-forget weapons which, once launched, find their own way to the target while the aircraft tries to return to its (nuclear blasted?) base.

Much of the effort on SOMs (stand-off missiles) has gone into guidance systems for steering towards a fixed target. Among the methods being used are pure inertial navigation, active mapping by radar or TV, terrain-comparison (called terrain-profile matching or terrain-contour matching), IIR (imaging IR) and digital scene-matching area-correlation which is a computerized way of comparing the scene viewed by the missile with 'scenes' stored in the ASM computer. None is the slightest use against an armoured division. Anti-tank missiles are covered in a separate chapter, but most of those weapons are fired by helicopters or slow aeroplanes and fly to their targets over substantially horizontal line-of-sight trajectories. ASMs also exist which pick out vehicles, especially tanks, from overhead. Yet other anti-armour, or anti-army, weapons are fired from defending ground launchers (including artillery) and home on targets illuminated or 'designated' by laser light or radar waves aimed by friendly aircraft which do not themselves carry weapons.

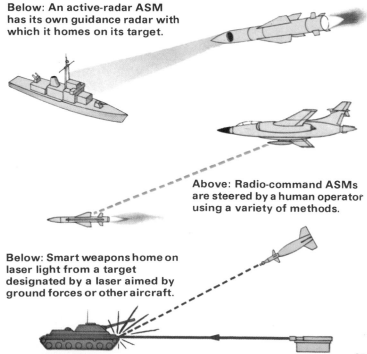

Below: An active-radar ASM has its own guidance radar with which it homes on its target.

Above: Radio-command ASMs are steered by a human operator using a variety of methods.

Below: Smart weapons home on laser light from a target designated by a laser aimed by ground forces or other aircraft.

ADSM

Origin: GD Pomona, USA.
Propulsion: Similar to, or derived from, that of Stinger: high-thrust launch motor and main-body sustain motor (see MLMS, p.38).
Dimensions: Not defined but rather longer and heavier than Stinger-POST (see MLMS, p.38).
Weight: At launch, about 30lb (13.6kg).
Performance: Not defined.
Warhead: Modified from that of BGT Viper.
Users: Expected eventually to include most NATO countries.

ADSM, (air-defence suppression missile), is a further variant of the infantry-fired Stinger SAM, and uses the same helicopter or fixed-wing launch installation as MLMS. The missile itself differs in having an extended nose guidance section with the POST (passive optical seeker technique) modified to use two-colour IR plus broadband RF aerials in two projecting probes extending well ahead of the glass seeker cover. The RF target designation system provides radar warning to the pilot of hostile radiating targets and cues the passive missile guidance on to that target. The complete dual-mode seeker had been fully tested by mid-1982, but funding for full development was still being sought. ADSM could be carried in groups of four by all tactical aircraft, a normal load being eight or 16.

Right upper: Hughes 500MD anti-tank Defender with mast-mounted sight, Black Hole Ocarina IR-suppressing jetpipes and ADSM boxes in place of anti-armour weapons.

Right: ADSM has a dual-guidance head and the Viper warhead.

Alarm

Among many other possibilities, which include RPVs used in the harassment role, British Aerospace Dynamics and MSDS (Marconi Space and Defence Systems) are attempting to develop the Alarm (air-launched anti-radiation missile), initially to meet British Air Staff Target 1228. Sky Flash proving fractionally too small to use as a basis, a slightly larger missile has been designed, but still considerably lighter than the US Harm, and thus capable of being carried in multiple by tactical aircraft in addition to a normal interdiction payload (for example, three rounds on each outboard pylon of Tornado). Configuration appears to resemble that of Sky Flash but with a larger body and considerably smaller wings and tail (because violent manoeuvres are not required). It has been reported that the weapon is fired as the aircraft approaches defended airspace, zooms up under the power of its two-stage solid motor to 40,000ft (12.2km) and then pitches over to point nose-down, the whole time under simple strapdown inertial guidance. It then falls slowly under a drogue parachute, whilst searching a large area for hostile emitters. The long search time ensures that every defence system in the area will be

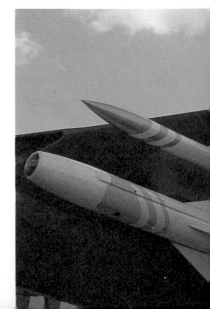

detected. The advanced micro-processor analyses the received signals and selects the most important target; the parachute is then jettisoned, the wings and tail flick open and the missile homes at high speed on to the selected radar. There are several features in which Alarm is ahead of all competing systems, but despite its very large export potential the British MoD is also studying the US Harm system, and is expected to choose between them by April 1983.

Below: BAe mock-up of Alarm with Martel, Sea Eagle, Sky Flash and SRAAM. Note comparative dimensions.

ALCM, AGM-86B

Origin: Boeing Aerospace Co, USA.
Propulsion: One Williams F107-101 turbofan with sea-level rating of 600lb (272kg) static thrust.
Dimensions: With wings/tailplane extended, length 20ft 9in (6.32m); body diameter 24.5in (620mm); span 12ft (3.66m).
Weight: At launch 2,825lb (1282kg).
Performance: Cruise speed 500mph (805km/h); range, varies with profile up to 1,550 miles (2500km).
Warhead: W-80 thermonuclear as originally developed for SRAM-B.
User: USA (Air Force).

Today potentially one of the most important weapons in the West's inventory, ALCM (Air-Launched Cruise Missile) was presented by President Carter as a new idea when he terminated B-1 as a bomber; he even said B-1 had been developed "in absence of the cruise missile factor", whose presence in 1976 made the bomber unnecessary. This is simply not true. The cruise missile never ceased to be studied from 1943, and—apart from such USAF examples as Mace and Snark—it was cruise-missile studies in 1963-66 that led to AGM-86 SCAD (Subsonic Cruise Armed Decoy) approved by DoD in July 1970. This was to be a miniature aircraft powered by a Williams WR19 turbofan, launched by a B-52 when some hundreds of miles short of major targets. Like Quail, SCAD was to confuse and dilute hostile defences; but the fact that some or all would carry nuclear warheads—by 1963 small enough to fit such vehicles—meant that SCAD could do far better than Quail. No longer could the enemy ignore the decoys and wait and see which were the bombers. Every SCAD had to be engaged, thus revealing the locations and operating frequencies of the defence sites, which could be hit by surviving SCADs, SRAMs or ARMs. SCAD was to be installationally interchangeable with SRAM, with a maximum range of around 750 miles (1207km). SCAD ran into tough Congressional opposition, but the USAF knew what it was about and in 1972 recast the project as ALCM,

retaining the designation AGM-86A. SCAD had had only a secondary attack function, but ALCM is totally a nuclear delivery vehicle, and like SRAM has the ability to multiply each bomber's targets and increase defence problems by approaching from any direction along any kind of profile. Compared with SRAM it is much easier to intercept, being larger and much slower, but it has considerably greater range and allows the bomber to stand off at distances of at least 1,000 miles (1609km).

The original AGM-86A ALCM was interchangeable with SRAM, so that a B-52G or H could carry eight on the internal rotary launcher plus 12 externally, and an FB-111A four externally plus two internally (though the latter aircraft has never been named as an ALCM carrier). This influenced the shape, though not to the missile's detriment, and necessitated folding or retracting wings, tail and engine air-inlet duct. Boeing, who won SCAD and carried across to ALCM without further competition, based ALCM very closely on SCAD but increased the fuel capacity and ▶

Below: AGM-86B No 10 (the last of the ten launched in the 1979 fly-off).

Above: Before building production ALCMs Boeing Aerospace had to make 20 perfect dummy AGM-86Bs, with correct mass distribution, to establish compatibility with the B-52G.

▶ the sophistication of the guidance, with a Litton inertial platform (finally chosen as the P-1000) and computer (4516C), updated progressively when over hostile territory by McDonnell Douglas Tercom (DPW-23). In 1976 the decision was taken to aim at maximum commonality with AGM-109 Tomahawk, but the guidance packages are not identical. The engine in both missiles is the Williams F107 of approximately 600lb (272kg) thrust, but in totally different versions; the ALCM engine is the F107-101, with accessories underneath and different starting system from the Dash-400 of AGM-109. The warhead is W-80, from SRAM-B.

AGM-86A first flew at WSMR on 5 March 1976. Many of the early flights failed—one undershot its target by a mile because its tankage had been underfilled!—but by the sixth shot most objectives had been attained and 1977 was spent chiefly in improving commonality with Navy AGM-109, in preparation for something unforeseen until that year: a fly-off against AGM-109 Tomahawk in 1979 to decide which to buy for the B-52 force. It was commonly said Boeing were told to make AGM-86A short on range to avoid competing with the B-1. In fact no more fuel could be accommodated and still retain compatibility with SRAM launchers, and in 1976 Boeing proposed an underbelly auxiliary fuel tank for missiles carried externally.

A better answer was to throw away dimensional compatibility with SRAM and develop a considerably stretched missile, called AGM-86B. This has a fuselage more than 30 per cent longer, housing fuel for double the range with a given warhead. Other changes include wing sweep reduced to 25°, thermal batteries for on-board electrical power, all-welded sealed tankage, improved avionics cooling and 10-year shelf life. President Carter's decision to cancel the B-1 in June 1977 opened the way for Boeing to promote this longer missile, which could still be carried externally under the wings of a B-52 but would not have fitted into the weapon bays of a B-1. From July 1979 Boeing's AGM-86B was engaged in a fly-off against GD's AGM-109. Results were hardly impressive, each missile losing four out of ten in crashes, quite apart from other mission-related failures, but after a long delay the USAF announced choice of Boeing on 25 March 1980. A month later it was announced that the USAF/Navy joint management was dissolved and that the USAF Systems Command would solely manage 19 follow-on test flights in 1980 and subsequent production of 3,418 missiles by 1987. The first two rounds assigned to SAC joined the 416th BW at Griffiss AFB in January 1981. Since then about half the 169 operational B-52G bombers have been converted to carry up to 12 rounds each, in two tandem triplets, and in 1982 President Reagan increased the buy to 3,780 missiles by 1990 to permit 96 B-52H bombers to be equipped also. From 1986 the internal bomb bays are to be rebuilt by Boeing-Wichita to permit each aircraft to carry a further eight rounds on an internal rotary launcher. Each B-52, after conversion, will have a permanently attached wing-root 'strakelet', visible in satellite pictures, as demanded by SALT II provisions. The pre-loaded wing pylons will be carried only in time of emergency.

The production B-1B will carry the same eight-barrel rotary launcher as the rebuilt B-52, and except for the first few aircraft will also carry a

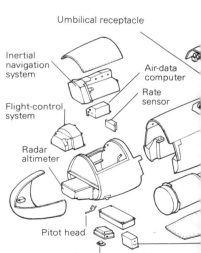

Umbilical receptacle

Inertial navigation system

Air-data computer

Rate sensor

Flight-control system

Radar altimeter

Pitot head

Radar altimeter aerial

Above: Test launch of a live AGM-86B from a B-52G of SAC. The missile is just unfolding its wings after dropping from the pylon under the left wing of the bomber (no right pylon fitted).

further 14 on eight external racks, making a total of 22. It is unlikely on present planning that any other aircraft in any NATO air force will carry the ALCM, though there would be no technical difficulty.

Below: AGM-86B showing the large internal fuel capacity which unfortunately destroyed compatibility with existing B-52 bomb bays and launchers.

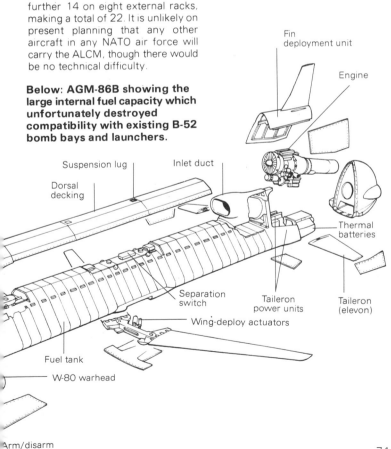

Fin deployment unit

Engine

Suspension lug

Dorsal decking

Inlet duct

Thermal batteries

Separation switch

Taileron power units

Taileron (elevon)

Wing-deploy actuators

Fuel tank

W-80 warhead

Arm/disarm

ANS

The Anti-Navire Supersonique (super-sonic anti-warship) is a new joint programme by Aérospatiale and MBB; in 1982 the French and West German governments were preparing an agreement for full-scale development. As the drawing shows, it will have ramjet propulsion to provide the four-times-higher thrust needed to cruise at wave-top height at twice the speed of, say, Exocet. MBB may manage the oxygen-lean fuel grain containing boron. The radar will have a digital processor.

AS-2 Kipper

Origin: Soviet Union.
Propulsion: One turbojet, believed to be a Lyul'ka AL-5F rated at about 12,000lb (5450kg).
Dimensions: Length about 31ft (9.5m); body diameter 35.4in (0.9m); span 16ft (4.88m).
Weight: At launch, about 10,000lb (4500kg).
Performance: Speed, generally considered to be marginally supersonic (Mach 1.2); range estimated from 132 to 350 miles (200-560km).
Warhead: Generally believed to be conventional, c.2,200lb (1000kg).
User: Soviet Union.

First seen at the 1961 Soviet Aviation Day display, this large ASM has a more advanced aeroplane configuration than the preceding—and now obsolete—AS-1 and is considerably larger, the Tu-16 Badger-C carrying one missile on the centreline recessed into the weapon bay. Propulsion is by a turbojet, possibly a Lyul'ka AL-5 in a short pod underslung at the rear. In appearance this missile faintly resembles Hound Dog, but is utterly different in mission, it being intended to attack moving targets with large radar signatures. Guidance probably duplicates that of AS-1, the new missile merely increasing flight performance and payload. Thus, it is believed to have simple autopilot mid-course guidance, until when in line-of-sight distance

AS-3 Kangaroo

Origin: Soviet Union.
Propulsion: One afterburning turbojet, possibly a Tumanskii R-11 or R-13 rated at about 15,000lb (6800kg).
Dimensions: Length about 48ft 11in (14.9m); body diameter 72.8in (1.85m); span 30ft (9.14m).
Weight: At launch, about 22,000lb (10 000kg).
Performance: Speed about Mach 1.8; range estimated at 400 miles (650km).
Warhead: Thermonuclear, nuclear or (unlikely) very large conventional, 5,070lb (2300kg).
User: Soviet Union.

This missile was also disclosed at the 1961 Soviet Aviation Day display, when one was carried low overhead by a Tu-20 (Tu-95) Bear bomber. This particular installation was probably a full-scale model to prove aircraft compatibility; the vehicle lacked many features seen in the actual missile, and a streamlined white nose appeared to be a temporary fairing forming part of the aircraft. This fairing is absent from some of the so-called Bear B and C carrier aircraft, many, if not all, of which belong to the AV-MF, the Soviet Naval Air Force. The missile is aerodynamically similar to Mach 2 fighters of the mid-1950s, and could well have been based on the Ye-2A Faceplate by the Mikoyan bureau. This was powered by a Tumanskii R-11 two-shaft afterburning turbojet rated at 11,244lb (5100kg), and this fits the missile perfectly. AS-3 has exactly the same wing, circular nose inlet, small conical centrebody,

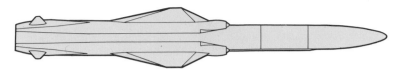

Above: Proposed ANS configuration; the four air intakes are to ensure a symmetrical flow to the ramjet's combustion chamber.

of a ship (possibly other) target it could home by its own active radar. The warhead is conventional and very large. Cruising speed has generally been estimated at Mach 1.2, at high altitude.

Above: One of the few available illustrations showing the large cruise missile known to NATO as AS-2 Kipper. It has just started its turbojet engine. Final dive will be at Mach 2+.

long instrument boom at the bottom of the nose, identical aerodynamic controls and the same fuselage structure, and the ventral fin at the rear resembles that of the earlier Mikoyan Ye-50 prototype. The tips of the tailplane have anti-flutter pods similar to those flown on the MiG-19 fighter but not fitted to Ye-2. AS-3 is commonly described as "operational since 1960" but was not seen in

Below: AS-3 Kangaroo is released from a Bear-B.

service until 1963. The main puzzle is how it steers itself to its target, because though it is easy to see how radio command/autopilot guidance could carry it up to 180 miles (290km) from the launch aircraft, despite cruising at Mach 2 with full afterburner, the ultimate range is put by the DoD at 350n.m., or 404 miles (650km) beyond the visual horizon. A nuclear warhead is assumed, and this suggests inertial or preprogrammed guidance against cities, ports and similar large fixed targets.

AS-4 Kitchen

Origin: Soviet Union.
Propulsion: Rocket, believed to be liquid propellant.
Dimensions: Length, about 37ft (11.3m); body diameter 35.4in (0.9m); span about 9ft 10in (3m).
Weight: At launch, about 13,000lb (5900kg).
Performance: Speed up to Mach 3.5 at high altitude; range variable up to 286 miles (460km) on all high-altitude profile.
Warhead: Nuclear 350 kiloton or large conventional, 2,200lb (1000kg).
User: Soviet Union.

Yet another disclosure at the 1961 Soviet Aviation Day fly-past was this much more advanced and highly supersonic ASM, carried recessed under the fuselage of one of the ten Tu-22 Blinder supersonic bomber/reconnaissance aircraft that took part.

This aircraft, dubbed Blinder B by NATO, had a larger nose radome, and other changes, as have several other Tu-22s seen in released photographs. Most aircraft of this sub-type have the outline of the AS-4 missile visible on their multi-folding weapon-bay doors, but the missile appears seldom to be carried today and in any case most remaining Tu-22s are of other versions, serving with the ADD and AV-MF. The missile itself has slender-delta wings, a cruciform tail and, almost certainly, a liquid-propellant rocket. Prolonged discussion in the West has failed to arrive at any degree of certainty concerning the guidance, though the general consensus is that it must be inertial, possibly with mid-course updating by a Tu-95 or other platform. A homing system is obviously needed for moving targets such as ships. Both versions of the swing-wing Tu-22M Backfire

Below: An excellent Swedish photograph of a Backfire-B (which deliberately posed for the purpose) carrying an AS-4 Kitchen.

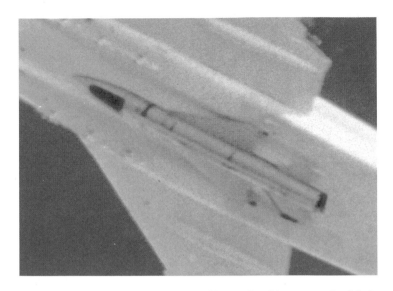

multi-role platform are believed to have carried this missile, probably in AV-MF service. Surprisingly, AS-4 has been seen on these new bombers frequently, whereas the later AS-6 has been seen more often on aged Tu-16 Badgers.

Above: Looking up at the AS-4 Kitchen recessed into the weapon bay of a Backfire. There are several types of this missile; this one is carried further forward than the different species seen below.

AS-5 Kelt

Origin: Soviet Union.
Propulsion: Single-stage liquid-propellant rocket with pump feed.
Dimensions: Length about 28ft 3in (8.6m); body diameter 35.4in (0.9m); span 15ft (4.57m).
Weight: At launch, about 6,600lb (3000kg).
Performance: Speed Mach 1.2 at high altitude (subsonic at low level); range up to 143 miles (230km) at high altitude (112 miles, 180km, at low altitude).
Warhead: Conventional, 2,200lb (1000kg).
Users: Egypt, Soviet Union.

First seen in a released photograph of September 1968, showing one of these missiles under the wing of a Tu-16, AS-5 is based on the airframe of AS-1 and some may even be rebuilds. In place of the turbojet and nose-to-tail duct there is a rocket with extensive liquid-propellant tankage. In the nose is a large radome. Superficially the nose and under-body fairing appear to be identical to those of the ship-launched SS-N-2 Styx and AS-5 thus is credited with the same choice of active radar or passive IR homing, having cruised to the vicinity of the target on autopilot, with initial radio-command corrections. By the early 1970s deliveries are thought to have exceeded 1,000, all of them carried by the so-called Badger G. This launch platform has the same pylons as the Badger B, and a nose navigator compartment.

AS-6 Kingfish

Origin: Soviet Union.
Propulsion: Rocket motor, said by US DoD to be solid-propellant.
Dimensions: Length about 33ft (10m); body diameter 35.4in (0.9m); span about 98in (2.5m).
Weight: At launch, about 11,000lb (5000kg).
Performance: Speed (DoD estimate), Mach 3 at high altitude; range (DoD) 155-350 miles (250-560km).
Warhead: Nuclear 350 kilotons or 2,205lb (1000kg) conventional.
User: Soviet Union.

At first thought to be a development of AS-4, this completely new missile gradually was reassessed as the first Soviet ASM publicly known that offers precision guidance over long ranges. It is still largely an enigma in the West, but has a very large fuselage with pointed nose, low-aspect-ratio delta wings and quite small aircraft-type tail controls. The fin is above the body, whereas in AS-4 it is on the underside. Propulsion is by an advanced rocket, and key features of AS-6 are much higher flight performance and dramatically better accuracy than any previous Soviet ASM. It clearly reflects vast advances in inertial guidance and nuclear-warhead design, and it is generally believed to possess terminal homing. According to the DoD one version has an active radar, while

Right: It is curious that most of the AS-6 Kingfish so far seen have been carried not by Backfires but by Badgers. This Badger-G was photographed by a Japanese F-86 in 1977.

In the early 1970s about 35 of these aircraft, plus missiles, were supplied to the Egyptian air force, possibly with Soviet crews and specialist tradesmen. In the Yom Kippur war in October 1973 about 25 missiles were launched against Israeli targets. According to the Israelis 20 were shot down en route, at least one by an F-4; five penetrated the defences. A supply dump was one of the targets hit, but at least two AS-5s homed automatically on to the emissions from Israeli radar stations. All the missiles were released at medium height of some 29,500ft (9000m), reaching a speed of about Mach 0.95; in the denser air at low level speed fell to about 0.85.

Below: Ageing Tu-16s of the Egyptian air force continue to tote their AS-5 Kelt ASMs.

another homes on enemy radar signals. Area-correlation has been suggested as a third (unconfirmed) possibility. Development appears to have been protracted, and though reported prior to 1972 AS-6 was still not in wide service in 1975. By 1977 it was carried under the wings of both the Tu-16 Badger-G and Tu-22M Backfire. User services certainly include the AV-MF and possibly the ADD. Launched at about 36,000ft (10973m) the missile climbs rapidly to about 59,000ft (17 983m) for cruise at about Mach 3. It finally dives on its target, or it can approach just above the sea or surface of the land.

AS-7 Kerry

Origin: Soviet Union.
Propulsion: Rocket, said by DoD to be single-stage solid-propellant.
Dimensions: No estimates yet published.
Weight: At launch (DoD estimate) 2,645lb (1200kg).
Performance: Speed, Mach 1; range up to 6.8 miles (11km).
Warhead: (DoD) conventional, 220lb (100kg).
User: Soviet Union, probably other countries soon.

Though the Soviet Union has clearly been testing tactical ASMs for at least 20 years, not one is known to have entered service until the late 1970s, a very strange fact. AS-7 was still almost completely unknown in the West in 1983, though for almost a decade it has been reported to be carried by the Su-24 Fencer, and it is probably part of the armament of the MiG -27 and several other FA (Frontal Aviation) types. Guidance was originally thought to be radio command, an outdated method which normally requires the directing aircraft to loiter in the vicinity of the target. In 1982 the DoD opinion was that AS-7 is a beam rider, though whether the beam is radar or laser has not been divulged. The traditional form of beam-riding guidance is a most odd choice for a missile intended to attack battlefield targets.

As this book goes to press it appears safer to regard the question of guidance as unknown. According to some reports it is carried by the Yak-36MP Forger, in this case presumably against ship targets.

AS-8

Origin: Soviet Union.
Data: Not available.

As yet not publicly associated with a NATO reporting name, this is said to be a "fire and forget" missile to be carried by all Soviet attack helicopters, such as the so-called Hind-D version of Mi-24 and the "A-10" gunship. Described as similar to the American Hellfire, it is reported to have a solid rocket motor, passive radiation seeker (Hellfire has a seeker that homes on laser radiation) and range of 5-6¼ miles (8-10km) at a flight Mach number of 0.5-0.8. IOC was apparently achieved in 1977 when AS-8 missiles began to appear on Mi-24 units in East Germany.

AS-X-9

Origin: Soviet Union.
Data: Not available.

Originally reported as an ARM (anti-radar missile) with a rocket motor for use from the Su-24 and similar FA tactical aircraft, AS-X-9 (called AS-9 in some 1982 American reports, indicating that it is now judged to be in combat service) is now known to be a large cruise-type weapon carried by the Tu-22 Blinder and Tu-16 Badger, and almost certainly by the Tu-22M Backfire. Recent DoD assessments describe it as a winged weapon with air-breathing (probably turbojet) propulsion, with a range of 62 miles (100km) at Mach 0.8 and carrying a 330lb (150kg) warhead. Other reports give it an even greater range of 124 miles (200km), which probably implies autopilot or strapdown inertial mid-course guidance before the seeker head locks on to a suitable emitting target.

AS-X-10

Origin: Soviet Union.
Data: Not available.

Another of the virtually unknown ASMs which have proliferated in US reports in the past few years, this is said to be an EO-homing (semi-active laser) precision missile, with a length of 10ft (3m), and a range of 6.2 miles (10km) at Mach 0.8 on the thrust of a solid rocket motor. Such a low speed seems odd for a weapon with such guidance intended to penetrate targets which are likely to be defended by modern weapons, and like the rest of the 'data' should be viewed with suspicion. Carrier aircraft are said to include the MiG-27, Su-17 and Su-24.

AS-11, -12

These are reported by the US DoD to be improved versions of AS-9, an ARM, with different homing heads and increased flight performance.

AS-X?

Origin: Soviet Union.
Data: Not available.
Also called ATASM, for Advanced Tactical ASM, this weapon is said to be a larger version of AS-X-10 with inertial or command mid-course guidance and EO-homing over the last part of its mission of up to 25 miles (40km) at high-subsonic speed. Presumably it will become AS-X-11 to the DoD and receive a NATO name.

AS-X?

Origin: Soviet Union.
Data: Not available.
This cruise missile with a range of 500 miles (800km) at Mach 3.5 (clearly indicative of air-breathing propulsion) is said to be in advanced development as a replacement for AS-6 Kingfish.

AS-X?

Origin: Soviet Union.
Data: Not available.

Possibly the result of indecision over the true range of the preceding weapon, this air-breathing cruise missile is said to have a range of 745 miles (1200km) and to be intended for the carriers of DA (Long-Range Aviation) such as the Bear and Backfire.

Below: Though not positively identified as AS-7 Kerry, the missile on the glove pylon of this Su-17 is probably it.

AS. 2L

Origin: SNI Aérospatiale, France.
Propulsion: SNPE solid motor (modified Roubaix or Lampyre) without boost charge.
Dimensions: Length 94.5in (2.4m); body diameter 6.3in (164mm); span (wings) 19.69in (500mm).
Weight: Approx: 132lb (60kg).

Performance: Speed about Mach 1.6; range variable to about 4 miles (6.5km).
Warhead: Not announced (different from Roland).
User: Not yet marketed.

This proposed missile is based on

AS. 11

Origin: SNI Aérospatiale, France.
Propulsion: SNPE boost/sustain solid motor.
Dimensions: Length 47.6in (1210mm); body diameter 6.3in (164mm); span 19.69in (500mm).
Weight: At launch 65.9lb (29.9kg).
Performance: Speed 360mph (580km/h); range 1,640-10,000ft (0.5-3km).
Warhead: Choice of Type 140AP02, detonates 5.72lb (2.6kg) charge after penetrating 0.4in (10mm) armour; 140AC, hollow charge which pierces 24in (610mm) armour; or 140AP59, contact-fuzed fragmentation.
Users: Have included France, UK, USA (designation AGM-22A) and 26 other countries.

Derived from the SS.11 army anti-tank missile, AS.11 is one of the oldest missiles still in operation. Originally developed by Nord-Aviation in 1953-5 as Type 5210, it has been slightly improved over the years, notably by the introduction of the AS.11B1 with transistorized circuits and optional TCA semi-automatic IR-based guidance, in 1962, and it stayed in production at Aérospatiale (into which Nord was merged) until late 1980, with deliveries exceeding 179,000 of all versions. The first

trials of an air-launched version were undertaken in France with Alouette IIs and in Britain using Twin Pioneers, in 1958. The weapon system is similar to that of the SS.11 but needs a stabilized sight and preferably an image intensifier or other magnifying all-weather vision system. Carrier aircraft include most versions of Alouette and Gazelle, the British Army Scout, Navy/Marines Wessex and various STOL aeroplanes. Though now obsolescent, AS.11 has been fired in at least 12 'wars' or other local conflicts, possibly a record for any ASM.

Right: An informative picture of the missile installation of an Alouette III light helicopter of the French ALAT (army light aviation). There are 4 launch units, AS 11 missiles being loaded on the outer pair. The replacement is the Hot missile which is launched from an Aérospatiale Gazelle.

the Roland SAM, but may eventually diverge from Roland in many respects. Though the Roland is a product of Aérospatiale and MBB it is purely a French project. The designation, sometimes written AS.LL, is from Air/Sol Léger Laser (air-to-surface lightweight laser), but from 1981 was seldom used, because shortage of funds is keeping the programme in a study phase. The guidance is closely similar to that of AS.30L and various French "smart bombs" with the Thomson-CSF Ariel seeker head. Compared with Roland, AS.2L would have a different airframe with fixed wings and fins, no boost motor, and completely different guidance. By mid-1982, after six years of study, there was no commitment from either government, and the programme seems to be moribund.

Above: Demonstration launch of AS.11 from an Alouette III. In this view the helicopter's roof-mounted stabilized sight can be seen.

AS. 12

Origin: SNI Aérospatiale, France.
Propulsion: SNPE boost/sustain solid motor.
Dimensions: Length 73.9in (1870mm); body diameter (max at warhead) 8.25in (210mm); span 25.6in (650mm).
Weight: At launch 168lb (76kg).
Performance: Speed 210mph (338km/h); range, max (measured relative to Earth) 5 miles (8km).
Warhead: Usually OP, 3C, explodes 63lb (28.4kg) charge after penetrating 1.57in (40mm) armour; alternative hollow-charge AP or fragmentation anti-personnel types.
Users: Include Abu Dhabi, Argentina, Brazil, Brunei, France, West Germany, Iraq, Iran, Italy, Ivory Coast, Libya, Netherlands, South Africa, Spain, Turkey, UK (RAF, RN), and ten other countries.

Developed in 1955-7 by Nord-Aviation, this missile was a natural extrapolation of the original SS.10 and 11 system to a bigger weapon, with a warhead weighing roughly four times as much and suitable for use against fortifications or ships.

Right: An AS.12 used by Nord-Aviation for display purposes in the 1960s, shown mounted on the launcher of an Alouette III of Sud-Aviation.

Trials began in 1958, and production of surface-launched SS.12 started in late 1959, with AS.12 following in 1960, the original planned carrier aircraft being the French Navy Etendard and Super Frelon. AS.12 can

AS. 20

Origin: SNI Aérospatiale, France.
Propulsion: SNPE boost/sustain solid motor.
Dimensions: Length 102.4in (2.6m); body diameter 9.84in (250mm); span 31.5in (800mm).
Weight: At launch 315lb (143kg).
Performance: Speed Mach 1.7; range 1.8-4 miles (2.9-6.5km).
Warhead: Conventional, 73lb (33kg) in early rounds, later standardized at 66lb (30kg).
Users: France, West Germany, Italy, South Africa.

France's first really successful AAMs were the R.511 and AA.20 (Nord

5103), and the command guidance of the latter was such that the operator in the launch aircraft could, if he was able to hold the target in view all the way to impact, steer the missile just as well to a surface target as into a hostile aircraft. Trials at Cazaux in 1958 confirmed this hope, and Nord accordingly developed the Type 5110 missile, adopted as AS.20, specially configured for ASM use. One of the main changes was to remove the proximity fuze and fit a simple impact fuze and any of four larger warheads. Details of the rest of the system are generally as for AA.20 (now obsolete), with guidance

be used with the APX 260 (Bézu) or SFIM 334 gyrostabilized sight and with IR night vision equipment, but the wire-transmitted guidance system is the basic CLOS type with optical (flare) tracking; the TCA semi-automatic IR command guidance system is not available with AS.12. Maximum airspeed at launch is 230 mph (370km/h). About 8,100 missiles had been produced by 1982, with deliveries then completed. AS.12 has been carried by the Alizé, P-2 Neptune, Atlantic, Nimrod, Alouette, Wasp, Wessex, Gazelle and Lynx. Several were fired by both sides in the Falklands war, one crippling an Argentine submarine at Grytviken.

by radio command, assisted by flares on the missile, and jet-deflection steering. Over 8,000 AS.20 missiles were delivered, and this missile was the first ASM used by European NATO air forces in 1961. Many remain in use as training rounds integrated with the AS.30 system and, with an adapter, fired from aircraft normally armed with AS.30. The radar-guided AS.25 did not progress beyond development.

Below: A standard production AS.20, many hundreds of which were fired in training missions from such aircraft as the G91, F-84, F-104 and Aquilon. Nord made 5,737 and MBB about 2,500.

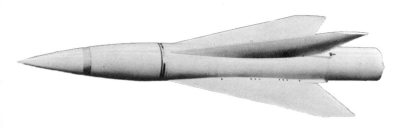

AS. 15TT

Origin: SNI Aérospatiale, France.
Propulsion: SNPE Anubis, Nitramite solid motor, smokeless, 45.2 sec burn time.
Dimensions: Length 85.04in (2.6m); body diameter 7.28in (185mm); span 22.22in (564mm).
Weight: At launch 220lb (100kg).
Performance: Speed over 628mph (1010km/h); range over 9.3 miles (15km).
Warhead: Derived from AS.12, conventional, 66lb (30kg).
Users: Saudia Arabia; other countries negotiating in 1982.

Though Lasso (AM.10) meets the requirements of the French Navy, it is right on the limits of what can be accomplished with wire guidance and could lose export sales to the British Sea Skua. To rival the British missile Aérospatiale is developing AS.15, in at least two versions, using the same warhead as AM.10 but with radio command guidance. The basic AS.15 has much in common with AM.10 but the body is slimmer and there are flip-out rear fins. It can be launched from existing AS.12 installations provided they have been updated to AM.10 standard with a stabilized sight and, preferably, Flir or imaging IR. Like other Aérospatiale tactical missiles of this series the basic AS.15 has to be steered all the way to the target by the operator. AS.15TT (Tous Temps, all-weather), on the other hand, is a substantially different missile, though again carrying the standard warhead. It is not roll-stabilized and is guided semi-automatically. The basic system de-

Below: The AS.15TT missiles on this AS.365F Dauphin helicopter are mock-ups, but a genuine live firing guided by the Agrion radar took place in late October 1982.

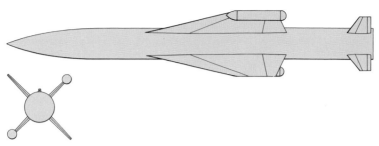

Above: Manufacturer's drawing of AS.15TT with two (now four) wingtip radar receiver pods. Development of this missile has been funded by the massive Sawari contract with Saudi Arabia.

pends on Thomson-CSF Agrion 15 radar (derived from the Iguane developed as a retrofit to the Alizé aircraft), with pulse-compression and frequency agility to improve behaviour in the presence of ECM. This radar continuously compares the sightlines to the target and missile, and a digital radio link drives the difference to zero. After a programmed descent to sea-skimming height on the radio altimeter the missile runs to within 1,000ft (300m) of the target and is then commanded to sink to immediately above the sea surface to be sure of hitting the target. AS.15TT has been integrated with two Aérospatiale helicopters, Dauphin 365N and the Super Puma. Both thus acquire a long-range surveillance capability with auto-digital link to the missiles or surface vessels. The first complete air-firing test, took place in October 1982.

AS. 30/30L

Origin: SNI Aérospatiale, France.
Propulsion: SNPE solid with composite boost and CDB sustainer (max time 21 sec).
Dimensions: Length (X12 warhead) 151in (3839mm), (X35) 153in (3885mm), (AS.30L) 143in (3650mm); body diameter 13.5in (340mm); span 39.4in (1m).
Weight: At launch 1,146lb (520kg).
Performance: Speed Mach 1.5; range up to 7 miles (11.25km).
Warhead: Conventional, 529lb (240kg), with optional impact or delay fuzes.
Users: (AS.30) France, West Germany, India, Peru, South Africa, Switzerland, UK (RAF); (30L) France and several (unannounced) export nations.

A logical scale-up of AS.20, this hard-hitting missile has a higher wing loading yet can be launched at Mach numbers down to 0.45 compared with the lower limit of 0.7 for the earlier missile. Originally the Nord 5401, it was developed in 1958 and disclosed on the Mirage III and Northrop N-156F in 1960. AS.30 was produced to meet a French DTE requirement for an ASM with range of at least 6.2 miles (10km) without the launch aircraft having to come within 1.86 miles (3km) of the target (today unacceptably close). CEP was to be 33ft (10m) or less, and all these demands were exceeded. Early AS.30 missiles, tested from Canberras and Vautours at Colomb-Béchar and Cazaux, were aerodynamically similar to AS.20. The missile is not roll-stabilized and the sustainer motor is equipped with two nozzles, one on each side. The operator keeps tracking flares on the missile aligned with the target by a radio link which sends signals to bias two vibrating spoilers that intermittently interrupt the jets from the nozzles. The autopilot interprets the command to interrupt the correct jet to steer left/right or up/down. In 1964 an improved AS.30 was produced with four flip-out tail fins indexed in line with the wings, and without spoilers on the sustainer nozzles. At the same time the TCA semi-automatic guidance system was introduced, with an SAT tracker in the aircraft continuously monitoring an IR flare on the missile and the pilot keeping the target centred in his attack sight, an on-board computer zeroing any difference between the two sightlines without the need to work a pitch/yaw joystick control. About 3,870 AS.30 missiles were delivered, most of them exported; only the Armée de l'Air used the TCA guidance.

As a company venture, Thomson-CSF and Aérospatiale began to work on a laser-guided AS.30 in 1974 (Ferranti in Britain proposed this with company hardware almost a decade earlier). Using Martin-Marietta licensed technology Thomson-CSF

Below: An AS.30L, with sustainer burning, immediately before hitting a target at Cazaux.

Above: The original AS.30 was a standard weapon of RAF Canberra squadrons. This AS.30 was carried by a B.6 at Akrotiri in the 1960s.

developed the Atlis (automatic tracking laser illumination system) target-designation pod and a complementary Ariel seeker head able to fit any missile of 3.94in (100mm) or greater diameter. Aérospatiale produced the AS.30L (AS.30 Laser) to make use of this more modern guidance system. In late 1977 an Armée de l'Air Jaguar A tested an Atlis 1 pod at

Below: This Jaguar A of l'Armée de l'Air was used for AS.30L trials with Atlis II.

Cazaux, in the course of which unguided AS.30L prototype missiles were fired. These had roll-stabilization and were programmed to fly on a gyro reference in a pre-guidance phase, prior to picking up the radiation from the target. In 1980 trials began using pre-production missiles homing on radiation from targets illuminated by the Cilas ITAY-7 1 laser in the Atlis 2 pod, which also includes a TV target tracker to assist accurate designation. In 1981 Aérospatiale claimed the system, linked with the Jaguar, was the only one in the world to allow autonomous firing with laser guidance from single-seat aircraft. Deliveries began in 1983, initially on 300 missiles to arm the last 30 Armée de l'Air Jaguars.

Asalm

Origin: No contractor selected, USA.

The US Air Force has for almost a decade recognised the size of the performance gap between existing strategic air-launched missiles and what is becoming possible, and in 1976 issued an RFP for the Advanced Strategic Air-Launched Missile. Generally written Asalm, pronounced as a word, all the submissions featured ram-rocket propulsion (integral rocket/ramjet) giving a cruising Mach number in the region of 3.5-4.5. This is fast enough for body lift to support the missile and give adequate manoeuvrability, so Asalm will probably have

---

ASM-1

Origin: Mitsubishi Heavy Industries, Japan.
Propulsion: Nissan Motors single-stage solid rocket.
Dimensions: Length 157.5in (4.0m); body diameter 13.75in (350mm); span 47.25in (1.2m).
Weight: At launch 1,345lb (610kg).
Performance: Speed Mach 0.9; range, maximum 56 miles (90km).
Warhead: Conventional anti-ship, 440lb (200kg).
User: Japan.

Mitsubishi was selected as prime contractor for this large anti-ship missile in 1973, and after successful development the basic air-launched version was accepted by the Defence Agency in December 1980. Work has also begun on other versions, including a surface-launched variant with a tandem boost motor and an extended-range model with turbojet propulsion. The basic ASM-1 has mid-course guidance provided by a Japan Aviation Electronics strapdown inertial system, with a TRT radio

---

ASMP

Origin: SNI Aérospatiale, France.
Propulsion: Integrated rocket/ramjet, probably using SNPE rocket with Statolite smokeless filling and Aérospatiale advanced kerosene-fuelled ramjet.
Dimensions: Length about 16ft 5in (5m); body diameter about 16.5in (420mm); width across inlet ducts about 32.2in (820mm).
Weight: At launch about 2,000lb (900kg).
Performance: Speed about Mach 4; range variable up to 186 miles (300km).
Warhead: CEA nuclear, 150 kilo-tonne.
User: France.

It is difficult to know whether to class this weapon as tactical or strategic, and the French are not sure themselves. Though it has a fair range, for the initials signify Air/Sol Moyenne Portée, it will have a nuclear warhead. ASMP was initiated in 1971 to arm whatever emerged as the next-generation Armée de l'Air deep-penetration aircraft, successively the Mirage G, ACF (Avion de Combat Futur) and Super Mirage. Cancellation of the latter in 1976 reduced the pace of development, and no deep-penetration platform is now in prospect. Development was initially competitive between Matra with turbojet propulsion, and Aérospatiale with a ram-rocket or ramjet. In March 1978 the go-ahead was given to Aérospatiale, with liquid-fuel ramjet propulsion. Today an integrated hybrid system has been

no aerodynamic surfaces except cruciform tail controls. Various arrangements of inlet and duct are proposed, a favoured inlet being in the chin position with a retractable or blow-off fairing to streamline the missile during the rocket boost phase. In mid-1978 the industrial teams most likely to develop Asalm were Martin Marietta with Marquardt propulsion and McDonnell Douglas with CSD (UTC) propulsion. Rockwell and Raytheon are among probable guidance contractors. With a range of several hundred miles, flown in about 10 minutes, Asalm is to be effective against all forms of surface target including those of the highest degree of hardening; it is also to be able to destroy Awacs-type aircraft. In late 1979 CSD ran a simulated mission test of the Asalm combustor and silica/phenolic nozzle. Lack of funding is a problem.

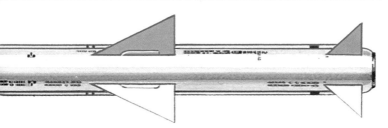

altimeter which holds altitude just above the tops of the largest waves. Near the target the Mitsubishi Electronics active radar seeker is switched on to home on to the largest reflective target. Guidance tests were flown with a C-1 transport in 1977, and in December that year unguided rounds were fired from an F-1 over Waseka Bay. Guided flight trials began in July 1978, at which time a US

Above: ASM-1 is a sea-skimmer with active radar homing, for use by the F-1 aircraft.

report gave the estimated unit price as $384,000. Production was initiated in late 1979, and from 1982 about 30 rounds per year are being delivered to F-1 squadrons. Other possible carrier aircraft include the P-2J and P-3C patrol aircraft.

chosen; France has only limited experience with such propulsion, and may licence technology from CSD, Vought, Marquardt, MBB or other company. Range specified for the original (January 1974) ASMP was 50-93 miles (80-150km). This has since been more than doubled, because of the short range of the only available carrier aircraft (Mirage IVA, 2000 and Super Etendard) and the chief puzzle now is how the

Above: ASMP mock-up on loading trolley. Note inlet duct.

Antilope 5 radar can acquire targets at over 186 miles (300km). Mid-course guidance is pre-programmed, with Sagem playing a major role in the main inertial guidance. About FF4.000 million is to be spent on 100 missiles which initially will be carried by Mirage IVA bombers from 1985.

AST. 1228

Origin: No contractor selected, UK.

Air Staff Target 1228 outlines a defence-suppression weapon to be carried by all aircraft called upon to penetrate heavily defended airspace. No indication has been given of the form of weapon suggested, and there has been speculation it could be a packaged harassment drone (RPV) which could confuse and dilute the hostile defence effort before finally homing on one of the defensive systems. Clearly, AST. 1228 demands a vehicle of minimum size, able to be carried (if possible in multiple) without seriously reducing other external pylon payloads.

Beluga

Origin: SA Matra, France.
Propulsion: None.
Dimensions: Length 130in (3.3m); body diameter 22.8in (580mm).
Weight: 639lb (290kg).

This weapon just qualifies for inclusion despite its lack of propulsion and guidance because of its general level of sophistication. A braked-bomb type container, released at up to 800mph (1290km/h) at heights as low as 200ft (90m), Beluga is a battlefield dispersion cluster package

**Right: Belugas on Jaguar A.
Each has 151 bomblets.**

containing Thomson-Brandt grenade-type submunitions. Three types of submunition can be fitted: anti-armour, general-purpose or area-saturation; and the area covered may be either 54,000ft² (5000m²) or 108,000ft² (10 000m²). The selection of area may be made by the pilot immediately prior to release. In all cases the impact trajectory is very nearly vertical to give maximum armour

Bullpup

Origin: Martin Marietta, USA (also Maxson and Kongsberg).
Propulsion: Prepackaged storable liquid rocket.
Dimensions: (AGM-12B) length 10ft 6in (3.2m); body diameter 12in (305mm); span 37in (940mm).
Weight: At launch (B) 571lb (259kg).
Performance: (B) Speed Mach 2.4; range 7 miles (11.3km).
Warhead: Conventional 250lb (113kg) GP bomb.
Users: Australia, Denmark, Norway, Turkey, UK, USA.

During the Korean War the US Navy urgently needed a precision ASM capable of being launched by carrier-based aircraft, and RFPs were issued in 1953. Martin Orlando Division's offering was chosen in May 1954, and subsequently was developed as ASM-N-7 Bullpup. It comprised a 250lb (113kg) bomb inside a roll-stabilized airframe with Aerojet-General solid motor, fixed rear wings, four pneumatically actuated nose control fins and twin rear tracking flares. The operator in the launch aircraft acquired the target visually, fired the missile and used a radio command joystick to impart left/right and up/down directions whilst keeping the flares lined up with the target as seen through his gunsight. It became operational in April 1959.

The existence of this primitive weapon at a price near $5,000 resulted in very wide acceptance. In 1960 it was replaced in production by N-7A, with Thiokol prepackaged LR58 acid/amine motor, extended- ▶

Right: AGM-12B Bullpups on prototype Skyhawk II (A-4H for Israel); all A-4 versions from the B of 1956 have had Bullpup capability (aircraft list, see text).

penetration. The Armée de l'Air have ordered an initial 1,500 Belugas for Jaguar and Mirage F1; the weapon has been cleared for F-5 and Alpha Jet and the Mirage 2000 will carry five or seven.

▶ range control and a new warhead. Re-styled AGM-12B in 1962, it was put into second-source production by W. L. Maxson, since 1963 US prime supplier for missiles, terminating at 22,100 rounds in 1970. Over 8,000 were built under licence by a European consortium headed by Kongsberg of Norway. Present carrier aircraft include the USN/USMC A-4, A-6, F-4, and P-3, and in Europe the F-4, F-5, F-100, F-104 and P-3.

In 1959 Martin Orlando developed an improved version for the Air Force with radio guidance that freed the operator from the need to align the target with his sight, allowing guidance from an offset position. This was produced as GAM-83A, and used by TAC. At the same time Martin developed two new versions. For the Navy ASM-N-7B (AGM-12C), Bullpup B, was a larger missile with 1,000lb (454kg) warhead, wings greatly extended in chord and Thiokol LR62 liquid motor; 4,600 were delivered. The Air Force adopted GAM-83B (AGM-12D) using an airframe closer to the original but with an increased-diameter centre section able to house either a conventional or nuclear warhead. The TGAM-83 (ATM-12A/B/D) Bullpup Trainer developed by Martin's Baltimore Division was later replaced by firing surplus AGM-12Bs with inert warheads. The final model was AGM-12E, briefly (840 rounds) built for the Air Force by Martin, with an anti-personnel fragmentation warhead.

There were several derived missiles intended to supplement or replace

Above: An early trials firing from an F-100D soon after USAF adoption of Bullpup.

the established models. Texas Instruments worked on Bulldog with EO (laser) guidance. Martin's AGM-79A Blue Eye competed with Chrysler's AGM-80A Viper, the former having a scene-correlation TV scanning system and Viper a strapdown inertial platform, both with warhead detonated by radio altimeter before impact.

Below: Firing an AGM-12B from an outboard wing pylon of a US Navy P-3B Orion.

Below: Four major production variants: from the rear, AGM-12C Bullpup B; AGM-12B Bullpup A; AGM-12D (nuclear warhead in fat section); and the ATM-12A Bullpup Trainer missile.

Carcara, MAS-1

Origin: Avibras-Industria Aerospacial, Brazil.

Since 1973 there have been repeated brief reports of this missile, said to have TV command guidance and capable of being carried by light attack aircraft such as the AT-26 Xavante. None has been seen in service.

CSW

Origin: No contractor yet selected, USA.

The proposed Conventional Stand-off Weapon is seen by many in the USAF as one of the best, if not the best, ways to destroy hostile anti-aircraft defences and armour moving forward behind the FLOT (forward line of troops, previously called FEBA). CSW is planned to be integrated with the Pave Mover synthetic-aperture SLAR (side-looking airborne radar) as now on evaluation in F-111 aircraft (competing radars are by Grumman/Norden and Hughes), and the PLSS (precision location strike system) is also available as an already deployed alternative carried in the TR-1 aircraft. In late 1982 there was still much argument over how best to engage distant armour, one of the major technical problems being how to give a radar such as Pave Mover the ability to discriminate between tanks and low-value trucks or even mobile decoys. No configuration for CSW has been announced, and the US Army is said to be undecided about offering parti-cipation or support. The USAF, however, sees CSW as a smaller and much cheaper back-up to MRASM (Medium-Range ASM, see page 118), with especial value in defence-suppression, and was hoping to initiate competitive development before 30 June 1983.

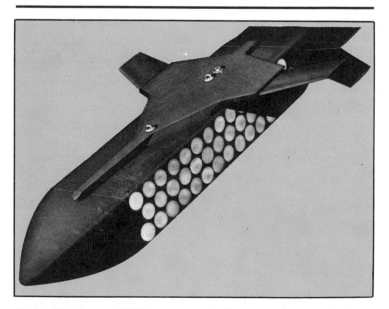

Above: Mock-up of CWS, whose variations are portrayed in the diagram at right which shows the customer options for nose and tail while preserving the standard 42-tube central container.

CWS

Origin: Messerschmitt-Bölkow-Blohm, West Germany.
Propulsion: (when fitted) one solid rocket motor.
Dimensions: Length 154in (3910mm), (with rocket) 163.4in (4150mm); body width 28.7in (728mm); body depth 16.5in (420mm); span (when fitted) 78.74in (2m).
Weight: At launch, (captive dispenser) 2,205lb (1000kg), (jettison) 2,425lb (1100kg), (stand-off) 2,646lb (1200kg), (standoff, powered) 3,307lb (1500kg).
Performance: Speed, high-subsonic; range (stand-off) up to 12.4 miles (20km).
Warhead: Dispenses submunitions.
User: Not yet marketed.

The Container Weapon System looks set to sell in large numbers as a purpose-designed system for dispensing bomblets for use against armour or other surface targets. Minimum cost and maximum versatility are assured by the modular concept, the one unvarying central feature being the 'warhead' comprising a container with 42 ejection tubes fired by an intervalometer. The submunitions are of the same types as previously produced for MBB's MW-1 simple dispenser used by German Tornados. To the central box may be added an upper hardback adapter fitting the NATO 30in (762mm) store station, or the same adapter fitted with wings for stand-off use. On the nose goes a fairing, or a fairing containing an autopilot and height sensor (set to 164 or 328ft, 50 or 100m), or containing these plus a 5/10km inertial platform, or these three units plus a computer. On the back goes a fairing which can have fins, or two powered control fins, or four (two-axis) control fins, or two-axis control plus the rocket.

CWS: Modular Units

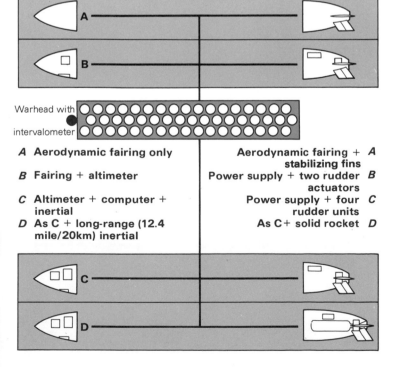

Warhead with intervalometer

A Aerodynamic fairing only

B Fairing + altimeter

C Altimeter + computer + inertial

D As C + long-range (12.4 mile/20km) inertial

Aerodynamic fairing + stabilizing fins *A*

Power supply + two rudder actuators *B*

Power supply + four rudder units *C*

As C + solid rocket *D*

Durandal

Origin: SA Matra, France.
Propulsion: SNPE Hector solid (Epictète-filled) smokeless motor.
Dimensions: Length 106.3in (2700mm); body diameter 8.78in (223mm); span 16.9in (430mm).
Weight: At launch 430lb (195kg).
Performance: Normally released at down to 185ft (56m) at up to 685mph (1100km/h).
Warhead: Conventional, 220lb (100kg), 1-sec delay fuze of 33lb (15kg) TNT charge.
Users: France and 11 other countries.

Originally gaining notoriety in 1969 as the 'concrete dibber' used by Israel, Durandal was developed in collaboration with SAMP as a weapon tailored to the task of causing maximum damage to concrete pavements and other hard targets such as concrete aircraft shelters. It is a simple tube which tactical aircraft can carry in multiple (16 on the Mirage 2000). After release it is braked by Matra's standard parachute braking kit (45,000 delivered) and tilted nose-down before the motor fires. Acceleration is extremely high, ground impact taking it through reinforced concrete 15.75in (400mm) thick before detonation of the warhead. Standard runway damage area is 2,153ft² (200m²). A single run by two aircraft is claimed to neutralize runway, taxiway, manoeuvring aprons and numerous shelters. Delayed-action fuzing is an option. By late 1982 well over 6,000 rounds had been sold, and Durandal was the winner of a long competitive evaluation by the USAF.

Right: Matra trials photograph showing a shower of Durandal pavement-penetrators in various stages of carriage, release, braking, nose-down pitch and motor ignition.

Below: Frame from a film taken during an early (c1972) trial with Durandals fired from a Mirage IIIR reconnaissance aircraft. No special aircraft gear is needed.

Exocet AM.39

Origin: SNI Aérospatiale, France.
Propulsion: Condor 2-sec boost motor and SNPE Hélios solid (Nitramite-filled) smokeless 150-sec burn sustainer.
Dimensions: Length 15ft 4½in (4690mm); body diameter 13.75in (350mm); span 43.3in (1.1m).
Weight: At launch 1,444lb (655kg).
Performance: Speed, high subsonic; range 31-43.5 miles (50-70km) depending on launch altitude.
Warhead: Serat hexolite/steel block, 364lb (165kg), penetrates armour at contact angles to 70°, proximity and delay fuzes.
Users: France and six other countries (not announced).

Exocet was designed as a ship-launched sea-skimming missile, fed with target data before launch and provided with inertial mid-course guidance, flying at Mach 0.93 at a height of about 8ft (2.5m), and finally switching on the EMD Adac X-band monopulse active radar seeker to home on the ship target. Exocet was obviously a potential ASM and inert rounds were dropped by an Aéronavale Super Frelon in April 1973, followed by cutgrain powered launches in June of that year. In May 1974 the decision was taken to put the air-launched Exocet into production for the Aéronavale, and since then Aérospatiale has sold this missile to an increasing list of export customers. Originally almost identical to MM.38, and designated AM.38, the ASM developed into AM.39 with a new propulsion system (see data) and reduced overall missile length and weight giving increased performance. The wings and fins are reprofiled to facilitate carriage at supersonic speeds, and because of the greater range and flight-time the Adac seeker radar operates over a greater angular scan. AM.39 entered Aéronavale service in July 1977 carried aboard the Super Frelon

(two missiles), followed by Pakistani Sea Kings. The Super Etendard followed in mid-1978 with either one or two on underwing pylons, and AM.39s fired from such aircraft of the Argentine navy gained world-wide notoriety in the Falklands conflict (the missile which hit HMS *Sheffield* failed to explode, the ship being lost due to a fire started by the still-burning sustainer). The successes have boosted an already good order-book, and new versions are under development. Aérospatiale claims AM.39 to be the only long-range missile in the West that can be launched from helicopters (the latest platform is the Super Puma). A one-second delay allows the missile to drop clear before boost-motor ignition.

Right: The sixth Super Etendard on carrier trails with an AM.39 Exocet under the right wing.

Above: Super Frelon helicopters of the French Aéronavale can carry two Exocets as alternative to four homing torpedoes. Designated SA.321G, they equip Flotille 32F at Lanvéoc-Poulmic.

French LGBs

Origin: SAMP and SA Matra, France.
Propulsion: None.
Dimensions: Similar to Paveway weapons.
Weight: Two production types have 2,205lb (1000kg) warheads, others being smaller.
Performance: Typical effective range up to 6 miles (10km).
Warhead: Usual sizes 551, 882 and 2,205lb (250, 400 and 1000kg).
Users: France and probably export customers.

Since the late 1970s SAMP and Matra, assisted by Thomson-CSF and other companies for guidance, have created French counterparts to the American Paveway series of LGBs (laser-guided bombs). All are matched to the Atlis II laser illuminator pod, and other lasers have been evaluated including types by Ferranti and Hughes. Seekers, packaged into the windvane-type nose guidance unit based directly on the Paveway weapons, include the Thomson-CSF Eblis and a Rockwell pattern. By 1981 large numbers of LGBs had

Gabriel III A/S

Origin: Israel Aircraft Industries, Lod, Israel.
Propulsion: Boost/sustain solid rocket motor.
Dimensions: Length 151in (3.84m); body diameter 13in (330mm); wing span 43in (1.1m).
Weight: c 1,322lb (600kg).
Performance: Speed, transonic; range over 37 miles (60km).
Warhead: Blast/frag 331lb (150kg), delay action fuze.
User: Israel.

The original family of Gabriel ship-launched missiles stemmed from various earlier weapons which included an air-launched version, and the wheel has now turned full circle with the perfection of Gabriel III A/S (air/surface). Autonomous after launch, it can be carried by F-4, F-16 or A-4 aircraft, and launched in either a fire-and-forget or a fire-and-update mode. In the latter the pre-programmed point in the sea-skimming run at which the inertial guidance is replaced by active radar homing is delayed to a point nearer the target, so the active search covers a smaller geographical sector and operates for a shorter time. IAI emphasize the excellent ECCM capability of Gabriel III and its exceptionally low cruise height which is set pre-launch according to sea state. Release for service could take place in 1983.

GBU-15, CWW

Origin: Rockwell International, USA.
Propulsion: None.
Dimensions: Length 154in (3.91m); body diameter 18in (457mm); span 59in (1499mm).
Weight: At launch 2,450lb (1111kg).
Performance: Speed, subsonic; range, typically 5 miles (8km) but highly variable with launch height and speed.
Warhead: Mk 84 bomb, 2,000lb (907kg).
Users: USA (AF) initially.

The CWW (cruciform-wing weapon) is the modern successor to the Vietnam-era Pave Strike Hobos (homing-bomb system), of which GBU-8 (guided bomb unit) was the chief production example. Like GBU-8, GBU-15 is a modular system comprising standard GP (general purpose) bombs to which a target-detecting device and trajectory-control fins are added. The full designation of the basic production missile is GBU-15(V)/B, and it is also called a modular guided glide bomb (MGGB) or modular guided weapon system. Though the payload and structural basis may be the CBU-75 cluster munition the normal basis is the Mk 84 2,000lb (907kg) bomb. To the front are added an FMU-124 fuze, a tubular adapter and either of two target-detecting devices, TV or IIR (imaging infra-red). At the rear

been produced in France and production deliveries had begun. In all cases the front guidance kit and flip-out rear wings can be adapted to standard bombs. Improved tracking results in miss-distances of 3ft (1m).

Above: A 500kg (1,102lb) LGB on wing pylon of a Mirage F1.C for export customer.

Above: GBU-15 on F-4 with Tiseo EO sensor above pylon.

are added an autopilot, displacement gyro, primary battery, control module and data-link module, and the weapon is completed by attaching four canard fins and four large rear wings with powered control surfaces on the trailing edges. (An alternative PWW, planar-wing weapon, by Hughes, is no longer active). GBU-15 is launched at medium to extremely low altitudes. In the former case it is guided over a direct line of sight to the target. In the latter it is launched in the direction of the target, while the carrier aircraft gets away at very low level. It is steered by a data-link by the operator in the aircraft who has a display showing the scene in the seeker in the nose of the missile (TV is the usual method). The missile climbs until it can acquire the target, and then pushes over into a dive. The operator has the choice of steering the missile all the way to the target or locking-on the homing head. Extensive trials from F-4, F-111 and B-52 aircraft are complete and substantial deliveries had been made by early 1983.

Harm, AGM-88A

Origin: Texas Instruments Inc, USA.
Propulsion: Thiokol single-grain (280lb, 127kg, filling of non-aluminized HTPB) reduced-smoke boost/sustain motor.
Dimensions: Length 13ft 8½in (4.17m); body diameter 10in (254mm); span 44in (1118mm).
Weight: At launch 796lb (361kg).
Performance: Speed over Mach 2; range/height variable with aircraft to about 11.5 miles (18.5km).
Warhead: Fragmentation with proximity fuze system.
Users: USA and UK, with several NATO countries in negotiation.

Neither Shrike nor Standard ARM is an ideal air-launched ARM and in 1972 the Naval Weapons Center began R&D and also funded industry studies for a High-speed Anti-Radiation Missile (Harm). Among the objectives were much higher flight speed, to lock-on and hit targets before they could be switched off or take other action, and to combine the low cost and versatility of Shrike, the sensitivity and large launch envelope of Standard ARM, and completely new passive homing using the latest microelectronic digital techniques and interfacing with new aircraft systems. In 1974 TI was selected as system integration con-

tractor, assisted by Hughes, Dalmo-Victor, Itek and SRI (Stanford Research Institute). The slim AGM-88A missile has double-delta moving wings and a small fixed tail. The TI seeker has a simple fixed aerial (antenna) yet gives broadband coverage, a low-cost autopilot is fitted, and Motorola supply an optical target detector forming part of the fuzing for the large advanced-design warhead. Carrier aircraft include the Navy/Marines A-6E, A-7E and F/A-18, and the Air Force APR-38 Wild Weasel F-4G and EF-111A, with

Below: General Dynamics put together these parts to create a proposed new Wild Weasel platform; F-16B two-seater; ALQ-131; tanks; two Harms; two Shrikes; and, on the tips, two self-defence Sidewinders.

Itek's ALR-45 radar warning receiver and Dalmo-Victor's DSA-20N signal analyser both interfaced. Proposed carriers include the B-52, F-16 and Tornado. Harm can be used in three modes. The basic use is Self-protect, the ALR-45 detecting threats, the launch computer sorting the data to give priorities and pass to the missile a complete set of digital instructions in milliseconds, whereupon the missile can be fired. In the Target of Opportunity mode the very sensitive seeker locks-on to "certain parameters of operation and also transmissions associated with other parts of a radar installation" which could not be detected by Shrike or Standard ARM. In the Pre-briefed mode Harm is fired blind in the direction of known emitters; if the latter are silent the missile self-destructs, but if one of them radiates, Harm at once homes on to it. Test flights began in 1976; redesign followed and following prolonged further tests delivery to user units began in early 1983.

Below: A production Harm on a USAF F-4G (with Advanced Wild Weasel badge also in picture). Harm is now operational on the F-4G EW and anti-SAM platform, with good results so far.

Harpoon, AGM-84A

Origin: McDonnell Douglas Astronautics, USA.
Propulsion: One Teledyne CAE J402-400 turbojet, sea-level thrust 661lb (300kg).
Dimensions: Length 12ft 7in (3.84m); body diameter 13.5in (343mm); span 30in (762mm).
Weight: At launch 1,160lb (526kg).
Performance: Speed Mach 0.75; range over 57 miles (92km).
Warhead: NWC 500lb (227kg) penetration/blast with impact/delay and proximity fuzing.
Users: USA (AF, Navy, Marine Corps); surface-launched and submarine versions widely exported, but no foreign sales announced for AGM-84A.

This potentially important weapon system began as an ASM in 1968, but three years later was combined with a proposal for a ship- and submarine-launched missile system. McDonnell Douglas Astronautics (MDAC) was selected as prime contractor in June 1971. The main development contract followed in July 1973, and of 40 prototype weapon systems 34 were launched in 1974-5, 15 being the RGM-84A fired from ships (including the PHM *High Point* whilst foilborne) and three from submarines, the other 16 being air-launched. At first almost wholly trouble-free, testing suffered random failures from late 1975, and the clearance for full-scale production was delayed temporarily. Production of all versions amounted to 315 in 1976, and about 2,100 by early 1983.

Target data, which can be OTH if supplied from a suitable platform, are fed before launch to the Lear-Siegler or Northrop strapdown inertial platform which can steer the missile even if launched at up to 90° off the desired heading. Flight control is by cruciform rear fins. A radar ▶

Right top: The first air-launched AGM-84A hung under a Navy P-3B Orion in May 1972. The P-3C still carries Harpoon.

Right: Four Harpoons, two Sidewinders and (just visible under the inlets) two Sparrows form a useful anti-ship mission load for the F/A-18A Hornet, seen at the St Louis plant.

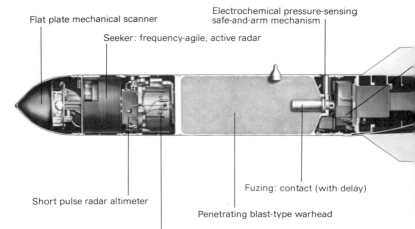

Flat plate mechanical scanner

Electrochemical pressure-sensing safe-and-arm mechanism

Seeker: frequency-agile, active radar

Short pulse radar altimeter

Fuzing: contact (with delay)

Penetrating blast-type warhead

Midcourse guidance unit: three-axis strapdown attitude reference assembly, general purpose digital computer

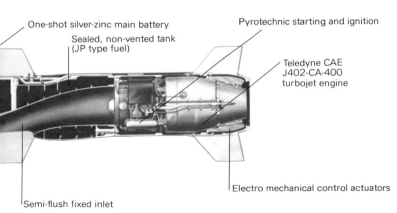

One-shot silver-zinc main battery

Sealed, non-vented tank
(JP type fuel)

Pyrotechnic starting and ignition

Teledyne CAE
J402-CA-400
turbojet engine

Semi-flush fixed inlet

Electro mechanical control actuators

Above: A McDonnell Douglas drawing showing salient features of AGM-84A air-launched Harpoon. No parts of the missile have to unfold after release.

Among the air-launch kit features are quick attack wings and fins, fore and aft launch lugs, warhead arming lanyard, and engine inlet duct and exit covers.

Right: ATM-84A is the air-launched training missile, seen on a wing pylon of a P-3C Update II of VP-23 squadron.

altimeter holds the desired sea-skimming height, and no link with the aircraft is required. Nearing the target the Texas Instruments PR-53/DSQ-58 active radar seeker searches, locks-on and finally commands a sudden pull-up and swoop on the target from above. The Naval Weapons Center and MDAC are also studying possible versions with supersonic speed, torpedo-carrying payload, imaging IR homing, passive radiation homing, nuclear warhead, vertical launch, midcourse guidance updating and other features.

MDAC expects to make at least 5,000 systems by 1988 despite the delayed start. Of these well over 2,000 will be for the US Navy, for surface ships, submarines, and P-3C, A-6E, S-3B, A-7E and F/A-18A aircraft, all of which should be cleared to use Harpoon by the end of 1983. The S-3 carries two missiles and the other types four. Production is at the rate of 40 missiles per month. Among the aircraft systems is a missile firing simulator.

Below: Frames from a film showing an AGM-84A Harpoon test against USS *Ingersoll*. The launch aircraft was an A-7C (the first of that variant) from China Lake; the ship was moored off Point Mugu.

HVM

Origin: Vought Corporation, USA.
Propulsion: Extremely rapid burn boost/sustain solid motor.
Dimensions: Not disclosed.
Weight: Under 50lb (27kg).
Performance: Speed 5,000ft/s (3,400mph, 5472km/h) within 0.6s of launch.
Warhead: None.
User: Not yet marketed.

Though primarily a ground weapon, the Hyper-Velocity Missile could later be fired from tactical aircraft, including helicopters. An anti-armour weapon, it kills purely by kinetic energy, the forebody containing a penetrator designed to pass through multiplate and other forms of advanced armour. The multi-tube launcher is boresighted on the target by an electronically scanned lidar (laser radar), and the extremely high missile speed reduces flight time to below 1 s, minimizing errors due to target motion or countermeasures. The system is all-weather.

Right: Ultrafast camera catches 2in HVM 0.01s after launch.

Indian ASM

Origin: A.D.E., India.
Propulsion: Microturbo TRI 60 turbojet, about 800lb (363kg) thrust.

It was announced in 1982 that the Indian government is seeking funds to develop this long-range cruise missile for use by such aircraft as the Jaguar and MiG-23. Guidance, and thus whether targets will be on sea or land, has not yet been hinted at.

Kormoran

Origin: MBB, West Germany.
Propulsion: SNPE double-base solid motors, twin Prades boost motors and central Eole IV sustainer.
Dimensions: Length 173.2in (4.4m); body diameter 13.39in (340mm); span 39.37in (1m).
Weight: At launch 1,323lb (600kg).
Performance: Speed Mach 0.95; range up to 23 miles (37km).
Warhead: Advanced MBB type, 352lb (160kg) with 16 radially mounted projectile charges and fuze delayed for passage through 3.5in (90mm) of steel plate.
Users: West Germany, Italy; later probably other countries.

The first major post-war missile programme in West Germany, this began life in 1964 to meet a Marineflieger (Navy Air) requirement for a large anti-ship missile. Based on a Nord project, the AS.34, using the Sfena inertial guidance planned for the stillborn AS.33, it became a major programme in the new consortium MBB, with Aérospatiale participation. The basic weapon exactly follows Nord/Aérospatiale principles, but incorporates more advanced guidance. After release from the F-104G or Tornado carrier aircraft the boost motors give 6,063lb (2750kg) thrust each for almost 1 sec, when the sustainer takes over and gives 628lb (285kg) for 100 sec. Sfena/Bodenseewerk inertial mid-course guidance is used with a TRT radio altimeter to hold less than 98ft (30m) altitude. The missile then descends as it nears the pre-inserted target position, finally descending to wavetop height as the Thomson-CSF two-axis seeker (operating as either an active radar or passive receiver) searches and locks-on. Impact should be just above the waterline, and the warhead projects liner fragments with sufficient velocity to penetrate up to seven bulkheads. Flight trials from F-104Gs began on 19 March 1970. The first of an initial 350 Kormoran production missiles was delivered in December 1977, and by mid-1978 the Marineflieger MFG 2 at Eggbeck was fully equipped. The first Tornado-Kormoran unit was MFG 1 at Schleswig-Jagel in 1982. It is also carried by Italian Tornados, and Boeing holds a US licence.

Below: Kormoran has from the start been the chief anti-ship missile of the Marineflieger. The F-104G seen here, from MFG 2 at Eggbeck, is being replaced by Tornado, which carries four missiles.

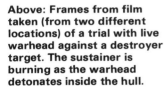

Above: Frames from film taken (from two different locations) of a trial with live warhead against a destroyer target. The sustainer is burning as the warhead detonates inside the hull.

Top of the page: The first air launch from an Italian Tornado took place over the NATO range at Decimomannu, Sardinia, in July 1978. In theory a Tornado could carry eight Kormorans, compared with two for F-104s.

JP. 233

Origin: Hunting Engineering, UK.
Propulsion: None.
Dimensions: Not disclosed.
Weight: (Largest size) in the region of 5 long tons (11,200lb, 5080kg).
Performance: Free fall.
Warhead: Payload of various bomblets.
User: Not yet adopted.

Originally known as the LAAAS (Low-Altitude Airfield Attack System), JP.233 is a series of submunition dispensers for parachute-retarded payloads which include pavement-cratering bomblets and anti-personnel mines, with or without delay-action fuzing. Aircraft with wing pylons can carry either short-finned containers for bomblets or medium-length finned containers for mines. The F-111 can carry a pair of each type, as can the F-16, but the Jaguar and Harrier can carry only one pair which must be of the same type. The most important carrier aircraft will be the Tornado IDS, which carries both types of payload in a single giant tandem pod on the centreline (which has significantly lower drag than the German MW-1 dispenser). Development began in November

Marte

Origin: Sistel—Sistemi Elettronici SpA, Italy.
Propulsion: SEP 299 solid boost motor (9,702lb, 4400kg, for 1.6s) and SEP 300 solid sustainer (220.5lb, 100kg, for 73s).
Dimensions: Length 15ft 5in (4.7m); body diameter 8.11in (206mm); span 39.37in (1m).
Weight: At launch 661lb (300kg).
Performance: Speed Mach 0.74; range over 12.4 miles (20km).
Warhead: Semi-armour-piercing, 154lb (70kg) with DA and proximity fuzes.
User: Italy.

This ASM system was initiated by the Italian Navy in 1967 to give aircraft an all-weather attack capability against surface warships. Sea Killer 2 was selected as the missile part of the system, and Sistel was appointed prime contractor. Major associates are Agusta, who provide the helicopter platform, and SMA for the MM/APQ-706 fire-control radar. Sea Killer is a sea-skimming missile with various forms of azimuth and terminal guidance. The usual carrier is the Agusta-built Sikorsky SH-3D, though Marte has been studied for smaller helicopters, notably the Italian Navy's AB212 (Marte has been tested on AB212s of the Argentine Navy). Smaller helicopters would carry only one missile and have no ASW capability. An SH-3D carries two missiles and the Marte system weighs a total of 2,568lb

Martin Pescador

Origin: CITEFA, Argentina.
Propulsion: Single-stage solid motor.
Dimensions: Length 9ft 7¾in (2.94m); body diameter 8.6in (218.5mm); span 28¾in (730mm).
Weight: At launch 308lb (140kg).
Performance: Speed Mach 2.3; range 1.5-5.5 miles (2.5-9km).
Warhead: Conventional 88lb (40kg) with DA fuze.
User: Argentina.

CITEFA, the armed forces scientific and technical research institute, claimed to have completed development of this tactical ASM in 1979, and one was displayed alongside an Agusta A109 helicopter at the 1981 Paris airshow. Performance given in the table is for launch from fixed-wing jet aircraft; from hovering helicopter launch the range is 2.7 miles (4.3km). It has simple line-of-sight radio command from the launch

Above: JP.233 tandem pod on a Tornado IDS. Two types of submunitions are dispensed.

1977 as a 50/50 programme with the USA, but the latter pulled out in 1982. Engineering development is due to be completed in 1984, by which time a decision may have been taken on which precision night and all-weather attack system to add to the carrier aircraft to ensure accurate laydown of payloads along runway centrelines.

Above: Marte (Sea Killer 2) firing from Italian Navy SH-3D.

(1165kg), made up of 600kg for the missiles, 400kg for the launch equipment and control console, 143kg for sonar and 22kg for the optical sight. The standard operational technique is for the radar to acquire a target at maximum range, the helicopter then descending to wave-top height and flying towards the target, finally popping up to re-acquire the target and launch the missile, which takes just over a minute to reach the hostile ship.

aircraft. None was used during the Falklands conflict in 1982. The name means Kingfisher.

Above: Martin Pescador on carry trials with an Aermacchi MB 326GB, 4 Esc, Argentine Navy.

Martel

Origin: Joint programme by SA Matra, France, and British Aerospace Dynamics (previously HSD).

Propulsion: Solid motor; (AS.37) SNPE Basile boost (2.4s burn) and Cassandre sustain (22.2s), both composite, (AJ.168) SNPE composite boost and cast double-base sustainer.

Dimensions: Length (AS.37) 162.2in (4.12m), (AJ.168) 152.4in (3.87m); body diameter 15.75in (400mm); span 47.25in (1.2m).

Weight: At launch (AS.37) 1,213lb (550kg), (AJ.168) 1,168lb (530kg).

Performance: Speed, see text; range (treetop-height launch) 18.6 miles (30km), (hi-alt launch) 37.2 miles (60km).

Warhead: Conventional 331lb (150kg) with DA or (AS.37) proximity fuze.

Users: France (AS.37 only), UK.

This excellent weapon grew from studies by HSD in Britain and Nord-Aviation and Matra in France in 1960-3. In September 1964 the British and French governments agreed to develop the weapon system jointly, in one of the first examples of European weapon collaboration. In the event it was Engins Matra that became the French partner, res-ponsible for the AS.37 anti-radar Martel. HSD developed the AJ.168 version with TV guidance. The name stems from Missile Anti-Radar TELevision.

Having a configuration similar to the AS.30, Martel has French propulsion. Flight Mach number is typically about 0.9, though this depends on angle of dive. Several sources state that Martel is supersonic.

The operator of AJ.168 studies the target area as seen on his control screen in the cockpit of the launch aircraft, fed by the MSDS vidicon camera in the nose of the missile. When he acquires a target he manually drives a small graticule box over it to lock-on the TV seeker before launch. The weapon is then fired, holding height constant by a barometric lock, and steered by the operator's control stick via a streamlined underwing pod which also receives the video signals from the missile. Special features assist the operator to steer the missile accurately to the target. AS.37 has an EMD AD.37 passive radiation seeker, with steerable inverse-Cassegrain aerial. If the rough location of a hostile emitter is known, but not its operating frequency, the seeker searches up and down a pre-set band of frequencies; when it detects the

Above: AJ.168 'British Martel' carried by Strike Command Buccaneer (note ARI.18228 radar warning pod on leading edge).

enemy radiation the aerial sweeps through 90° in azimuth to pinpoint the location. When it has locked-on the missile is launched, thereafter homing automatically. Alternatively, if the hostile radiation is known before takeoff the seeker can be fitted with a matched aerial and receiver to pinpoint the source. AS.37 continues to home no matter how the hostile radiation may change frequency so long as it remains within the preset band.

Both versions of Martel have the same warhead, AS.37 having a Thomson-CSF proximity fuze. AS.37 is carried by the Mirage III, Jaguar,

Buccaneer and Atlantic; AJ.168 is used only by the RAF Buccaneers, but could be made compatible with the Phantom, Tornado and two-seat Jaguar or Harrier, and has been mentioned in a weapon list for Nimrod. Production terminated in the late 1970s.

Below: AS.37 'French Martel' carried by Mirage IIIE of the Armée de l'Air.

Maverick, AGM-65

Origin: Hughes Aircraft, USA.
Propulsion: Thiokol boost/sustain solid motor, from 1972 TX-481 and from 1981 TX-633 with reduced smoke.
Dimensions: Length 98in (2490mm); body diameter 12in (305mm); span 28.3in (720mm).
Weight: At launch (AGM-65A, shaped-charge) 463lb (210kg), (65A, blast/frag) 635lb (288kg).
Performance: Speed classified but supersonic; range 0.6-10 miles (1-16km) at sea level, up to 25 miles (40km) after Mach 1.2 release at altitude.
Warhead: Choice of Chamberlain shaped charge (83lb, 37.6kg, charge) or Avco steel-case penetrator blast/frag.
Users: Include Egypt, Greece, Iran, Israel, South Korea, Morocco, Saudi Arabia, Sweden, Turkey, USA; West Germany, Italy, UK negotiating for later versions.

Smallest of the fully guided or self-homing ASMs for US use, AGM-65 Maverick was approved in 1965 and, following competition with Rockwell, Hughes won the programme in June 1968. An initial 17,000-missile package was fulfilled in 1975, and production has continued at reduced rate on later versions. The basic missile, usually carried in triple clusters under the wings of the F-4, F-15, F-16, A-7, A-10 and Swedish AJ37A Viggen, and singly by the F-5 and the BGM-34 RPV, has four delta wings of very low aspect ratio, four tail controls immediately behind the wings, and a dual-thrust solid motor.

In mid-1978 Hughes completed production of 26,000 AGM-65A Mavericks and for three years had no production line. The pilot selects a missile, causing its gyro to run up to speed and light a cockpit indicator. The pilot then visually acquires the target, depresses his uncage switch to remove the protective cover from the missile nose, and activates the video circuitry. The TV picture at once appears on a bright display in the cockpit, and the pilot then either slews the video seeker in the missile or else lines up the target in his own gunsight. He depresses the track switch, waits until the cross-hairs on the TV display are aligned on the target, releases the switch and fires the round. Homing is automatic, and the launch aircraft at once escapes from the area. Unguided flights began in September 1969. AGM-65A has been launched at all heights down to treetop level. In the 1973 Yom Kippur war it was used operationally, in favourable conditions. It requires good visibility, and the occasional $48,000 A-model breaks its TV lock and misses its target—for example, because of overwater glint.

AGM-65B, Scene-Magnification Maverick, has new optics, a stronger gimbal mount and revised electronics. The pilot need not see the target, but instead can search with the seeker and cockpit display which presents an enlarged and clearer picture. Thus he can identify the target, lock-on and fire much quicker and from a greater slant range. AGM-65B was in production (at up to 200 per month) from May 1980 to May 1983. AGM-65C Laser Maverick was for close-air support against laser-designated targets, the lasers being the infantry ILS-NT200 or the ▶

Above: Maj John Bland of the US Marine Corps looks at the first AGM-65E Laser Maverick to be launched by the corps; it was also the first firing from an A-4 (A-4M) and the third of the laser weapon.

Below: Regular AGM-65A Maverick has from the start been cleared for all TAC aircraft in the attack mission, some of the F-16 trials being flown with the first F-16B two-seater shown here.

▶airborne Pave Knife, Pave Penny, Pave Spike, Pave Tack or non-US systems. Flight testing began in January 1977, using the Rockwell tri-Service seeker. Troop training has established the method of frequency and pulse coding to tie each missile to only one air or ground designator, so that many Mavericks can simultaneously be homed on many different sources of laser radiation. AGM-65C was replaced by AGM-65E with 'tri-Service' laser tracker and digital processing which in 1982 was entering production for the US Marine Corps with heavy blast/frag warhead. Westinghouse tested Pave Spike with the Minneapolis-Honeywell helmet sight for single-seat aircraft.

In May 1977 engineering development began on AGM-65D IR-Maverick, with Hughes IIR tri-Service seeker. Considerably more expensive than other versions, the IIR seeker—especially when slaved to an aircraft-mounted sensor such as FLIR, a laser pod or the APR-38 radar warning system—enables the Maverick to lock-on at least twice the range otherwise possible in northwest Europe in mist, rain or at night. Of course, it also distinguishes between "live targets" and "hulks". Using the centroid seeker in place of the original edgelock optics, AGM-65D was tested from an F-4 in Germany in poor weather in January-March 1978. While Hughes continues to produce the common centre and aft missile sections, delay with the laser-seeker E-version means that AGM-65D got into pilot production first.

All AGM-65A Mavericks have the same 130lb (59kg) conical shaped-charge warhead, but different war-

Above: This colourful missile was one of the early AGM-65A development rounds, seen here under an Air Force A-7D Corsair II. Aerodynamically Maverick was derived from the Falcon.

heads are in prospect. The Mk 19 250lb (113kg) blast/fragmentation head is preferred by the Navy and Marines, giving capability against small ships as well as hard land targets, and may be fitted to C and D versions with new fuzing/arming and a 4 in (102mm) increase in length. Another warhead weighs 300lb (136kg), while in December 1976 the Air Force expressed a need for a nuclear warhead.

Hughes' Tucson, Arizona, plant is likely to be hard-pressed to handle TOW, Phoenix and residual Roland work on top of enormously expanded Maverick production. By far the largest numbers are expected to be of the IIR Maverick, AGM-65D, of which well over 30,000 rounds are predicted at a rate of 500 per month. Prolonged tests have confirmed the long range, which at last matches the flight limitations of the missile itself, and AGM-65D is the standard missile for use with the Lantirn night and bad-weather sensor system now being fitted to F-16s and A-10s. The Navy is expected to procure AGM-65F, which is almost the same missile but fitted with the heavy penetrator warhead of AGM-65E, and with modified guidance software exactly matched to give optimum hits on surface warships. With this missile family Hughes has achieved a unique capability with various guidance systems and warheads, resulting in impressively large production and interchangeability.

Below: Launch of one of a triple cluster of AGM-65As from the first F-16B in July 1979. Dive attacks are not essential and the launch aircraft can turn away.

MRASM, AGM-109

Origin: General Dynamics Convair Division, USA.
Propulsion: Modified Teledyne CAE J402-400 turbojet (660lb, 300kg, sea-level thrust).
Dimensions: Length (H,K) 234in (5.94m), (I) 192in (4.88m); body diameter 21in (533mm); span (wings extended) 103in (2.616m).
Weight: At launch (H) 2,900lb (1315kg), (I) 2,225lb (1009kg), (K) 2,630lb (1193kg).
Performance: Speed 550mph (885km/h); range (sea level, Mach 0.6) (H) 293 miles (472km), (I) 350 miles (564km), (K) 316 miles (509km).
Warhead: (H) 58 TAAM bomblet/mine payloads, 1,060lb (481kg); (I) WDU-7B or -18B unitary warhead, 650lb (295kg); (K) WDU-25A/B unitary warhead, 937lb (425kg).
User: USA.

The General Dynamics AGM-109 was one of the chief versions of the Tomahawk strategic nuclear cruise missile, first tested in air drops from P-3 Orions and A-6 Intruders in 1974. It differed from the ship/submarine/GLCM versions in having no rocket boost motor or launch capsule/box. Main propulsion, at first a J402, switched like other versions to a Williams F107 turbofan in competition with the Boeing AGM-86B as the ALCM for SAC.

When the Boeing missile was chosen, Tomahawk was recast in different roles, and eventually in 1981 the naval versions were all terminated, chiefly on cost grounds. GLCM continued as a tactical weapon of the Air Force, and a completely new version, MRASM (Medium-Range ASM) was launched in 1981 as a non-nuclear cruise missile for wide use by the Air Force arming many types of aircraft beginning with the B-52 and F-16. Though in early 1983 still not given a full go-ahead by Congress, which for two years has looked at alternative delivery systems, MRASM has been taken to a high pitch of development—interestingly enough with the original pure-jet engine, but in a much modified form able to fly 8-hour missions burning the new JP-10 fuel and with a positive oil storage, retapered turbine, oxygen start system and zirconium-coated combustor. The basic missile has been developed in three forms, differing in payload and guidance. AGM-109H is the baseline airfield attack missile, with DSMAC II (digital scene-matching area-correlation) guidance and carrying a heavy payload of 58 TAAM (tactical airfield attack missile) bomblets or mines, discharged from upward-facing tubes along the fuselage. This version is in competition with short-range or free-fall anti-

Below: Specially prepared for this book, this cutaway shows the basic features of AGM-109I MRASM, which is also known as GD Tomahawk II. It stemmed from a 1,500-mile strategic ALCM.

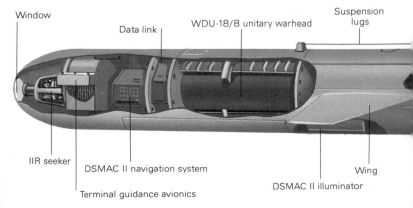

Window
Data link
WDU-18/B unitary warhead
Suspension lugs
IIR seeker
DSMAC II navigation system
Terminal guidance avionics
Wing
DSMAC II illuminator

airfield weapons, and justifies its high cost by the fact it is a launch-and-leave missile which eliminates the need for the carrier aircraft to come within 300 miles (483km) of the target. AGM-109I is a dual-role weapon proposed to the Navy for use by A-6E squadrons. It has a large unitary warhead and both DSMAC II and IIR (imaging IR) guidance for either anti-ship or land attack missions.

Above: General Dynamics makes both the F-16B and Tomahawk II MRASM shown at the AF Flight Test Center.

AGM-109K is a pure sea-control missile with only IIR guidance; the scene-matching and large fuel-cell power plant are replaced by an enlarged warhead. GD states that all versions could have IOC in 1985.

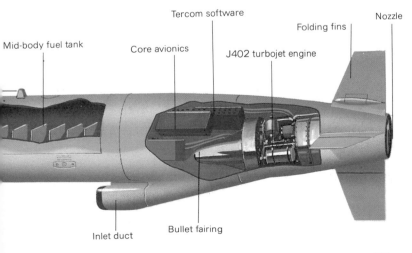

Tercom software

Nozzle

Folding fins

Mid-body fuel tank

Core avionics

J402 turbojet engine

Inlet duct

Bullet fairing

NATO FALW

In 1982 NAFAG (NATO Air Force Armaments Group) was continuing discussions to try to increase multinational standardization with a Family of Air-Launched Weapons. These cover various AAMs (including Asraam and AMRAAM and ASMs, including a long-range SOM standoff missile (only MRASM is suitable), a SRARM (Short-Range ARM) for defence suppression over ranges of some 19 miles (30km) and a larger ASM of some 62 miles (100km) range.

ND-7

Though by late 1982 it had not been exhibited, ND-7 has for at least two years been a privately funded programme at Northrop for a cruise missile able to fly launch-and-leave anti-airfield missions. Smaller and very much cheaper than MRASM, ND-7 comprises a streamlined lightweight container with rocket propulsion and inertial guidance, almost certainly augmented by some extra fine-tuning guidance to allow it to fly down runway centrelines in the most adverse conditions. In 1981 MBB of West Germany was collaborating, possibly on payload dispenser engineering.

P4T

Since 1980 BAe Dynamics has been studying this long-range cruise missile which was initially derived from Sea Eagle (p.128). In its basic form it would be powered by the same TRI.60 turbojet, but since early 1981 parallel studies have been made of a supersonic-cruise model powered by the TRI.80 or Microturbo/ Turboméca SS engine for cruise at up to Mach 1.8. Guidance would be by Terprom (terrain profile matching, similar in principle to the US Tercom) with final terminal homing by any of various possible seekers on the design of which MSDS, Ferranti and BAe itself have been working. Various unitary and runway-cratering dispensed payloads have been studied.

Paveway LGBs

Origin: Texas Instruments, USA.
Propulsion: None.
Dimensions: As for original bombs plus from 6 to 20in (152-500mm) length and with folding tailfins.
Weight: As for original bombs plus about 30lb (13.6kg).
Performance: Speed, free-fall; range, free-fall so varies with release height, speed.
Warhead: As in original bombs.
Users: Include Australia, Canada, Greece, South Korea, Netherlands, Saudi Arabia, Taiwan, Turkey, UK (RAF, RN), USA (AF, Navy, Marines).

This code-name identifies the most diverse programme in history aimed at increasing the accuracy of tactical air-to-surface weapons. This USAF

effort linked more than 30 separately named systems for airborne navigation, target identification and marking, all-weather/night vision, weapon guidance and many other functions, orginally for the war in SE Asia. In the course of this work the "smart bombs" with laser guidance managed by the Armament Development and Test Center at Eglin AFB, from 1965, were developed in partnership with TI, using the latter's laser guidance kit, to form an integrated family of simple precision weapons. The first TI-guided LGB was dropped in April 1965.

By 1971 the Paveway I family of guidance units had expanded to eight, in six main types, of which the three most important were the KMU-388 (based on the 500lb, 227kg, Mk82 bomb), KMU-421 (1,000lb 454kg, Mk83) and KMU-351 (2,000lb, 907kg, Mk84).

All these bombs are extremely simple to carry, requiring no aircraft modification or electrical connection; they are treated as a round of ordnance and loaded like a free-fall bomb. Carrier aircraft have included the A-1, A-4, A-6, A-7, A-10, A-37, F-4, F-5, F-15, F-16, F/A-18, F-100, F-105, F-111, AV-8A, B-52 and B-57. Targets can be marked by an airborne laser, in the launch aircraft or another aircraft, or by forward troops. Like almost all Western military lasers the matched wavelength is 1.064 microns, the usual lasers (in Pave Knife, Pave Tack or various other airborne pods) being of the Nd/YAG type. More recently ▶

Below: Carry trials of Paveway II by an F-5E Tiger II. On the centreline is a GBU-10E/B. and the wing weapons are GBU-12D/B.

Above: Original Paveway I British 1,000lb bomb on MoD trials Buccaneer XW986.

▶ target illumination has been provided by the Atlis II, LTDS, TRAM, GLLD, MULE, LTM, Lantirn and TI's own FLIR/laser designator.

In all cases the guidance unit is the same, the differences being confined to attachments and the various enlarged tail fins. The silicon detector array is divided into four quadrants and is mounted on the nose of a free universal-jointed housing with an annular ring tail. As the bomb falls this aligns itself with the airstream, in other words the direction of the bomb's motion. The guidance computer receives signals from the quadrants and drives four control fins to equalize the four outputs. Thus, the sensor unit is kept pointing at the source of laser light, so that the bomb will impact at the same point. Electric power is provided by a thermal battery, energised at the

moment of release, and power to drive the fins comes from a hot-gas generator.

Users include the RAF for use on Mk 13/18 1,000lb (454kg) bombs carried by Buccaneers, Tornados and Jaguars. Total production of Paveway guidance units has been very large; in the early 1970s output was at roughly 20,000 per year, at a unit price of some $2,500. Since 1980 the Paveway II weapons have been in production including a simpler and cheaper seeker section, and a folding-wing aerofoil group. Portsmouth Aviation has integrated the system with RAF bombs used from Harriers over the Falklands. Paveway III has flick-out lifting wings and a microprocessor and can be dropped at treetop height. It is due to enter production in 1983. BAe Dynamics supplies the Dart precision gyro.

Below: KMU-351 (2,000lb bomb) hitting dummy driver of target truck in firing trials.

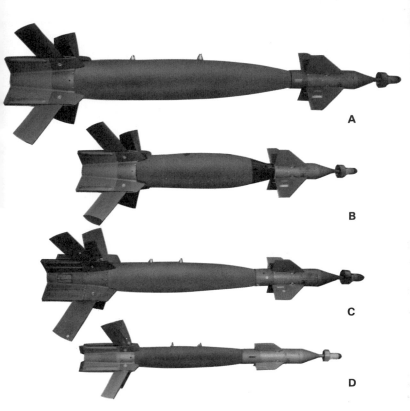

Above: Today the production at Texas Instruments is centred on the Paveway II family, which feature several important changes which improve performance and reduce cost. A, the GBU-10E/B, based on the 2,000lb Mk 84 bomb (replaces KMU-351A/B). B, Mk 13/18 is fitted to the British 1,000lb GP bomb. C, GBU-16B/B is based on the Mk 83 1,000lb GP bomb (replacing KMU-421B). D, GBU-12D/B is based on the Mk 82 GP bomb of nominal 500lb size. In turn these will progressively switch to Paveway III weapons.

Below: Early Paveway II test missiles on YF-16 No 2 in 1974. All sizes are cleared for use on the production F-16 family.

Penguin

Origin: A/S Kongsberg Väpenfabrikk, Norway.
Propulsion: Raufoss solid sustainer motor.
Dimensions: Length 10ft 5¼in (3.18m); body diameter 11in (280mm); span 39.37in (1m).
Weight: At launch 765lb (347kg).
Performance: Speed over Mach 0.8; range variable with launch speed/height up to max over 25 miles (40km).
Warhead: As Bullpup, 250lb (113kg) bomb, DA fuze.
User: Norway.

Penguin was developed by Kongsberg and the Norwegian Defence Research Establishment as a ship-to-ship weapon in the 1960s. From it was derived Penguin Mk 3 for air launching, with smaller wings, no boost motor and higher flight performance. It is basically a simple weapon, readily adaptable to fighter-type aircraft and launched from a standard Bullpup pylon. Mid-course guidance is inertial, followed by terminal homing by an IR seeker or a PEAB active radar. Another version is to home on hostile emissions using a passive seeker. BAe Sperry Gyroscope produce the canard actuation system and Saab-Scania of Sweden the launcher and system power unit to be installed in KNL (Royal Norwegian AF) F-16s which are to become operational with Penguin 3 in 1987. As initial development was completed in 1974, including carry trials on F-104Gs, this seems a very long timescale, but the missile itself has undergone successive modifications.

Right: Early Penguin 3 mounted on KNL F-104G for carry-trials in 1974 (not operational).

RB 05A

Origin: Saab Bofors Missile Corporation, Sweden.
Propulsion: Volvo Flygmotor VR-35 liquid rocket motor, 5,620lb (2550kg) boost, 1,124lb (510kg) sustain.
Dimensions: Length 11ft 10in (3.6m); body diameter 11.8in (300mm); span 31.5in (0.8m).
Weight: At launch 672lb (305kg).
Performance: Speed supersonic; range up to 5.6 miles (9km).
Warhead: Conventional warhead by Forenade Fabriksverken, proximity fuzed.
User: Sweden.

When the decision was taken to restrict what had been the Robotavdelningen (national missile directorate) to R&D only, Saab was the natural choice for this missile, prime responsibility for which was placed with the company in 1960. Originally known as Saab 305A, RB 05A is a simple command-guidance weapon readily adaptable to many types of launch aircraft. One unusual feature is supersonic flight performance, conferred by advanced aerodynamics and a pre-packaged liquid motor fed with Hidyne and RFNA, pumped by

Right: RB 05A with pylon adapter for left-hand body fitting on AJ 37A during 1976 trials.

a gas-pressurized piston and collapsible aluminium bladder to burn rapidly in a boost phase and slower in the sustainer mode. Motor performance is independent of missile attitude or acceleration, and there is no visible smoke. The missile rapidly overtakes the launch aircraft and automatically centres itself dead ahead; it is then steered by a micro-wave link from the pilot's miniature control stick. The guidance is claimed to be highly resistant to jamming, able to control the missile at low altitudes over all kinds of terrain, and able to attack targets at large offset angles. RB 05A is carried by the AJ37A Viggen and can be carried by other Swedish aircraft including the SK60 trainer.

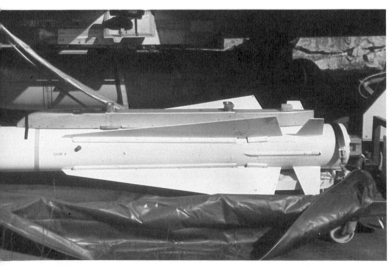

RB 04

Origin: Saab (now Saab Bofors), Sweden.

Propulsion: Solid rocket motor with boost/sustain charges fired consecutively.

Dimensions: Length 14ft 7in (4.45m); body diameter 19.7in (500mm); span (RB 04C, D) 80.3in (2.04m), (E) 77.5in (1.97m).

Weight: At launch (C,D) 1,323lb (600kg), (E) 1,358lb (616kg).

Performance: Speed high-subsonic; range variable with launch height up to 20 miles (32km).

Warhead: Unitary 661lb (300kg) conventional, DA and proximity fuzes.

User: Sweden.

This hard-hitting ASM has enjoyed one of the longest active programmes of any guided missile, for the requirement was finalized in 1949, and missile hardware was being manufactured for 28 years (1950-78). Planned as a primary weapon to be carried by the Saab A32A Lansen, this missile was originally designed and developed by the Robotavdelningen (guided-weapons directorate) of the national defence ministry, whose first missile, RB302, was flight-tested in 1948 from a T18B bomber. The original RB (Robotbyrån) 04 was made large enough to carry an active radar seeker, giving all-weather homing guidance earlier than for any other ASM apart from Bat. The configuration is of aeroplane type, with a rear delta wing with end fins and four control fins around the forebody. The two-stage solid cast-DB motor is by IMI Summerfield Research Station in Britain. The radar is by PEAB (Swedish Philips) and the autopilot, originally the XA82, is a Saab design with pneumatically driven gyros and surface servos. The first launch took place from a Saab J29 fighter on 11 February 1955, and following very successful development the first production version, RB 04C, entered service with the Swedish Air Force in 1958, equipping all A32A

aircraft of attack wings F-6, -7, -14 and -17. In the early 1960s the Robotavdelningen developed a version with improved motor and guidance, RB 04D, which was in production in the second half of that decade. On 1 July 1968 the bureau became part of the Air Materiel department of the Försvarets Materielverk (Armed Forces Materiel Admin, FMV), and the ultimate development of this missile, RB 04E, was assigned to Saab (now Saab Bofors). Produced mainly to arm the AJ37 Viggen, which carries up to three, RB 04E has a reduced span, modernised structure and more advanced guidance. All versions have the same very large fragmentation warhead.

Right: RB 04E missiles carried by an AJ 37 Viggen of Flygvapen wing F15 based at Söderhamm.

Above: An RB 04E development missile mounted on the centreline pylon of an AJ 37 retained by Saab-Scania as a trials platform.

RBS 15F

Origin: Saab Bofors Missile Corporation, Sweden.
Propulsion: Microturbo TRI 60-2 Model 077 turbojet, sea-level thrust 831lb (377kg).
Dimensions: Length 171.25in (4.35m); body diameter 19.7in (500mm); span 55in (1.4m).
Weight: At launch 1,318lb (598kg).
Performance: Speed high-subsonic; range, classified but several tens of kilometres.

Warhead: Large FFV blast/fragmentation with DA and proximity fuzes.
User: Sweden.

RBS15 was designed as a ship-to-ship weapon for use aboard the *Spica II* FPBs. In August 1982 Saab Bofors announced a Swedish defence materiél administration (FMV) order, worth some SK500 million, for the RBS15F air-launched version, for use by Viggens and the forthcoming

Sea Eagle

Origin: British Aerospace Dynamics, UK.
Propulsion: Microturbo TRI 60-1 Model 067 turbojet, sea-level thrust 787lb (357kg), mainly made in UK.
Dimensions: Length 13ft 5½in (4.1m); body diameter 15.75in (400mm); span 47.25in (1.2m).
Weight: Classified but clearly in the 1,200lb (550kg) class.
Performance: Speed, probably about Mach 0.9; range, classified but several tens of miles.
Warhead: ROF product, suitable to disable the largest surface warships.
User: UK (RAF, RN).

Originally designated P3T, Sea Eagle is an over-the-horizon fire-and-forget missile developed from Martel by switching to air-breathing propulsion and adding active radar and sea-skimming capability. Launched to meet Air Staff Requirement 1226, it progressed swiftly to the project definition phase in 1977, and development has been remarkably trouble-

free. The airframe is basically that of Martel, with an underbelly air inlet. Guidance is initially on autopilot, with the on-board microprocessor storing the target's last known position and velocity, with height maintained by a Plessey radar altimeter just above the waves (or following a programmed profile). The target is then acquired by the very advanced MSDS active radar seeker. Electric power comes from Europe's first production lithium batteries. Features include full night and all-weather capability against the most powerful and electronically sophisticated targets, low life-cycle costs and 'round of ammunition' storage and maintenance. Launch trials began in ▶

Right: Four Sea Eagles on the trials Buccaneer XK527, which was uniquely built as an S.1 and converted to an S.2. Note the fairings over the engine inlet and nozzle to reduce drag.

JAS. The 15F has no launch canister or boost motors, but is carried on external pylons and launched when over the horizon from the target. A fire-and-forget weapon, it has pre-programmed mid-course guidance and an advanced radar seeker by PEAB with digital processing and frequency agility, selectable search patterns and modes, target-choice logic (to pick the most important of a group of hostile ships) and variable ECCM facilities. Saab announced RBS 15 will have quick reaction time, high kill probability and high efficiency against all naval targets in any weather. IOC will probably be in about 1986.

Below: One of the chief RBS 15F carrier aircraft will be the Saab 39 (JAS), seen with the missile on its inboard pylon.

▶November 1980, and a full-range sea-skimming flight was made in April 1981. In early 1982 a £200 million production contract—a fixed-price incentive agreement—was announced. Sea Eagle will enter service in the mid-1980s, initially on RAF Buccaneers (four missiles) and RN Sea Harriers (two). It can be carried by all other tactical aircraft and is almost certain to be issued to RAF Tornado GR.1 squadrons. It is also seen as the basis for a long-range missile for use against high-value land targets. P5T is a proposed ship-fired version.

Left: An unusual air-to-air photograph of the first fully guided Sea Eagle in the sea-skimming mode on its highly successful flight in autumn 1982. The engine air inlet can be seen between the lower pair of wings.

Below: Sea Eagle is well suited to the Sea Harrier, and to variants of the AV-8B/Harrier 5. The latter could carry four, but two missiles will be a normal load for Fleet Air Arm Sea Harrier FRS.1s.

Sea Skua

Origin: British Aerospace Dynamics, UK.
Propulsion: BAJ Vickers solid boost/sustainer motors.
Dimensions: Length 98.5in (2.5m); body diameter 9.75in (250mm); span 28.5in (720mm).
Weight: At launch 320lb (145kg).
Performance: Speed high subsonic; range over 9.3 miles (15km).
Warhead: Blast/frag, 44lb (20kg), exploded within ship hull.
User: Initially UK (RN).

Originally known by its MoD project number of CL-834, this missile is significantly more advanced than the comparable French missiles being developed as successors to AS.12. Instead of having wire or radio command guidance Sea Skua is based on semi-active radar homing, and in its first application aboard the Lynx helicopter the target is illuminated by the specially developed Ferranti Seaspray overwater radar. The RN Lynx is equipped with this surveillance/tracking radar, as well as fire-control equipment and launchers for four missiles. The weapon system is intended to confer upon helicopter-armed frigates and similar surface ships the capability to destroy missile-carrying FPBs, ACVs, PHMs and similar agile small craft at ranges greater than that at which they can launch their own missiles. This range is also said to be great enough to provide the launch helicopter with considerable stand-off protection from SAMs. The Decca Tans navigation system of the Lynx can combine with ESM cross-bearings to identify and fix the target, backing up the position on the Seaspray display. The Sea Skua, treated as a round of ammunition needing only quick GO/NO GO checks, is then launched and swoops down to one of four pre-selected sea-skimming heights, depending on wave state, using a BAe-manufactured TRT radio altimeter. Near the target a pre-programmed or command instruction lifts the missile to target-acquisition height for the MSDS homing head to lock-on. Guided trials began in 1978 and

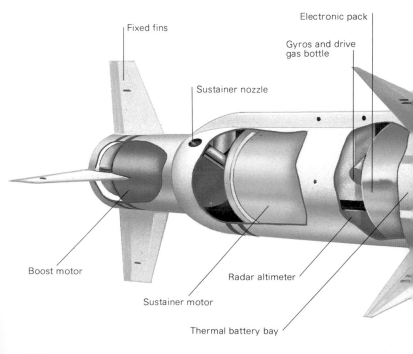

Fixed fins

Electronic pack

Gyros and drive gas bottle

Sustainer nozzle

Boost motor

Radar altimeter

Sustainer motor

Thermal battery bay

BAe has privately financed studies matching Sea Skua to other aircraft (including fixed-wing) and in coast-defence installations. BAe expect that this missile, roughly one-tenth as heavy as Exocet but able to cripple the radars and weapon launchers of all known targets, and to destroy ships of 1,000 tons with one shot, will find very wide use. In

Above: Four Sea Skuas carried by a Lynx HAS.2. Development was speeded to allow operational deployment over the Falklands.

the Falklands on 2 May 1982 two Lynx each ripple-fired a pair of Sea Skuas, sinking an 800-ton warship and crippling another, despite appalling weather and heavy seas.

Below: Simplified cutaway of Sea Skua showing the tandem boost/sustainer motors, cruciform guidance wings and forward warhead and radome.

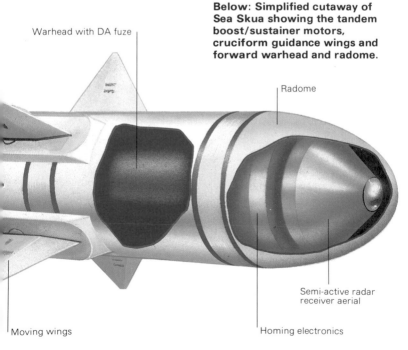

Warhead with DA fuze

Radome

Semi-active radar receiver aerial

Moving wings

Homing electronics

133

Shrike, AGM-45

Origin: Naval Weapons Center (NWC), with production by TI, USA.
Propulsion: Rockwell (Rocketdyne) Mk 39 or Aerojet (ATSC) Mk 53 (polybutadiene) or improved Mk 78 (polyurethane, dual-thrust) solid motor.
Dimensions: Length 120in (3.05m); body diameter 8in (203mm); span 36in (914mm).
Weight: At launch (approximately depending on sub-type) 390lb (177kg).
Performance: Speed Mach 2; range 18-25 miles (29-40km).
Warhead: Blast/frag, 145lb (66kg), proximity fuze.
Users: Include Iran, Israel and USA (AF, Navy, Marines).

Based in part on the Sparrow AAM, this was the first anti-radar missile (ARM) in the US since World War 2. Originally called ARM and designated ASM-N-10, it was begun as a project at NOTS (later NWC) in 1961, and in 1962 became AGM-45A. Production by a consortium headed by Texas Instruments (TI) and Sperry Rand/Univac began in 1963 and Shrike was in use in SE Asia three years later with Wild Weasel F-105Gs and EA-6As. Early experience was disappointing and there have since been numerous models, identified by suffix numbers, to rectify faults or tailor the passive homing head to a new frequency band identified in the potential hostile inventory. Carried by the US Navy/Marines A-4, A-6, A-7 and F-4, the Air Force F-4, F-105 and EF-111 and the Israeli F-4 and Kfir, Shrike is switched on while flying towards the target and fired as soon as the TI radiation seeker has locked-on. After motor cutoff Shrike flies a ballistic path until control-system activation. The seeker has a monopulse crystal video receiver and continually updates

Below: An early test launch of a prototype Shrike on 12 June 1964, the aircraft being an A-4C. Externally this round looks much like that shown above.

Above: AGM-45A Shrike typical of the final production series.

the guidance by determining the direction of arrival of the hostile radiation, homing the missile into the enemy radar with its cruciform centre-body wings driven in 'bang/bang' fashion by a hot-gas system. There were at least 18 sub-types in the AGM-45-1 to -10 families, with over 13 different tailored seeker heads, of which the USAF bought 12,863 by 1978 and the Navy a further 6,200. In the Yom Kippur war Israel used Shrike tuned to 2965/2990 MHz and 3025/3050 MHz to defeat SA-2 and SA-3 but was helpless against SA-6. In 1978-81 additional procurement centred on the -9 and -10 for the USAF to be carried by F-4G and EF-111A platforms, together with modification kits to equip existing rounds to home on to later SAM and other radars.

SRAM, AGM-69

Origin: Boeing Aerospace, USA.
Propulsion: Originally Lockheed Propulsion Co two-pulse solid motor; Thiokol is in low-rate production with a long-life motor with numerous improvements.
Dimensions: Length (with tail fairing for external carriage) 190in (4.83m), (without fairing) 168in (4.27m); body diameter 17.5in (444.5mm); span (three fins at 120°) each tip is 15in (381mm) from axis of missile.
Weight: At launch 2,230lb (1012kg).
Performance: Speed Mach 2.8-3.2; range (very variable depending on launch height and selected profile) 35-105 miles (56-169km).
Warhead: Nuclear W-69, 200 kT, air burst and DA fuzes.
User: US (AF).

Throughout the 1950s nuclear warheads became ever smaller, and by 1960 studies showed that a missile that could be carried by a fighter could deliver a large nuclear warhead from a range exceeding 100 miles (161km). In the event the SRAM (Short-Range Attack Missile) has not been used by fighters, but by aircraft of SAC, primarily to neutralise potential hostile defences such as radars, SAMs and other AA systems. The adjective "short-range" has taken on a new meaning, while the compact lightweight design of this high-performance weapon multiplies in dramatic fashion the number of targets that one bomber can engage. Boeing, the final prime contractor, began SRAM studies in December 1963, ahead of the drafting of SOR-212 in 1964 which resulted in the establishment of WS-140A. A keen competition followed in 1965, with selection in November 1965 of Boeing and Martin and final choice of Boeing (now Boeing Aerospace Co) on 31 October 1966. A dummy SRAM was dropped from a B-52 in December 1967, live flights began in 1969, and IOC was reached in early 1972. Production of 1,500 AGM-69A missiles was completed in July 1975, the missile then equipping 18 SAC bases operating the B-52G and H and FB-111A.

Originally there were to be different guidance systems, Sylvania supplying a radar-homing version and an IR-homer also being required. These were not procured, and AGM-69A has only inertial guidance by Singer-Kearfott, with a Delco on-board computer to command very varied flight profiles. Four basic trajectories are: semi-ballistic; terrain-following; pull-up from "under the radar" followed by inertial dive; and combined inertial and terrain-following. The small, almost perfectly streamlined missile is said to have a radar cross-section "about as large as a bullet". ▶

Right: Despite its range of more than 100 miles (161km) SRAM is a modest weapon, because of diminution in size of warheads. Here 4 test missiles are on the external pylons of an FB-111A.

Above: USAF 60-0062 was the Boeing B-52H that was used for SRAM compatibility testing during the missile's evaluation. Here the four external triplets are clearly visible.

▶The B-52 can carry eight on a rotary launcher reminiscent of a revolver cylinder in the aft bomb bay (exceptionally, and at the expense of other loads, it can carry three such launchers internally), plus two tandem triplets on each former Hound Dog pylon, modified for SRAM compatibility, a total of 20 missiles. The FB-111A can carry up to six, four on swivelling wing pylons and two internally. The bombardier selects each missile in turn, checks the updating of the KT-76 inertial guidance and lets it drop. The motor accelerates it to about Mach 3, fast enough to fly and steer with body lift and three tail fins (there are no wings). Nearing the target the second propulsion stage is ignited.

About 1,300 missiles remain available to SAC's dwindling forces. AGM-69B, an improved missile with nuclear hardening throughout, the W-80 warhead, a completely new

Above: FB-111A with weapon-bay open showing SRAM on left.

Thiokol HTPB-propellant motor and greatly increased computer memory, was almost ready for production for the B-1, which can carry 32; AGM-69B was cancelled in 1977 following discontinuance of the production programme for B-1. The remaining A-series missiles must, however, be fitted with the new Thiokol motor, because of ageing problems, and computer-memory and nuclear-hardening improvements are also projected. There is no money for production of new missiles, despite attractions of large carrier aircraft such as the 747-200F which could carry 72 internally. Originally the size of SRAM dictated the dimensions of ALCM (p.68) but the latter is now much longer. There is no announced intention to produce extra SRAMs for the B-1B.

Left: A B-52G-100 of SAC (ship 0-58-204) with production AGM-69As carried externally. Each has an aerodynamic tail fairing, and aircraft drag and range are not much affected.

Above: Eight rounds loaded on the rotary launcher installed in the aft bomb bay of a SAC B-52G. ALCM (AGM-86B) was meant to fit this launcher, but it grew much too long.

Standard ARM, AGM-78

Origin: General Dynamics Pomona Division, USA.

Propulsion: Aerojet (ATSC) Mk 27 Mod 4 boost/sustain solid motor.

Dimensions: Length 180in (4.57m); body diameter 13.5in (343mm); span (rear fins, greater than strake wings) 43in (1.09m).

Weight: At launch, typically 1,400lb (635kg).

Performance: Speed Mach 2.5; range (depending on launch height) up to 35 miles (56km).

Warhead: Conventional blast/fragmentation, direct-action and proximity fuzes.

Users: South Korea, USA (AF, Navy, Marines).

In September 1966 the Naval Air Systems Command contracted with Pomona Division of General Dynamics for an ARM having higher performance, longer range and larger warhead than Shrike, which at that time was giving indifferent results. Unlike Shrike the whole programme was developed in industry, the basis being the Standard RIM-66A ship-to-air missile. Flight testing took place in 1967-8; production of AGM-78 Mod 0 began in late 1968 and ten years later had absorbed well over $300 million at a unit price initially in the neighbourhood of $128,000. AGM-78 Mod 0 was carried by the Air Force Wild Weasel

F-105F and G and the Navy A-6B and E. The missile flies on a dual-thrust motor, steering with tail controls and very low aspect ratio fixed wings. The Mod 0 AGM-78A of 1968 was fitted with the TI seeker used in Shrike. This was soon replaced by the Maxson broad-band seeker of the main (Mod 1) production version, AGM-78B. This has capability against search, GCI, SAM and other radar systems, and is intended to give the launch platform freedom to attack from any direction and turn away "outside the lethal radius of enemy SAMs". Carrier platforms preferably have a TIAS (Target Identification and Acquisition System) able to measure "specific target parameters" and supply these to the seeker head in the missile before launch. The Mod 1 missile is compatible with the APR-38 system carried by the USAF F-4G Wild Weasel which supplies this need. AGM-78C, D and D-2 have further-increased capability and reduced unit cost, but in 1978 production was not funded, (deliveries then about 700) and effort has since been devoted to improving missiles with field mod kits. Navy and Marine A-6E squadrons carry this missile, as would the Wild Weasel F-16.

Below: AGM-78 Standard ARM is seen here under the left-wing of a USAF F-4G Advanced Wild Weasel Phantom together with an AGM-45A Shrike, ALQ-119 ECM pod (recessed in Sparrow mount) and 600-US gal tank.

Stand-Off Missile

Since 1980 there has been increasingly urgent discussion within NATO, especially within the European air forces, to develop a new conventional SOM to enable interdiction aircraft, such as Tornado and the F-111, to

STM

Origin: Vought Corporation, USA.
Propulsion: UTC Chemical Systems Division integral rocket/ramjet, with Naval Weapons Center solid boost grain.
Dimensions: Not disclosed but about 190in (4.8m) long and with body diameter 17in (432mm).
Weight: Not disclosed but in 2,000lb (907kg) class.
Performance: Has demonstrated flights over 100 miles (161km) at sustained speed of 2,000 mph (3220km/h, Mach 2.7).

Following an earlier LVRJ (low-volume ramjet) programme Vought has achieved good results under Navy contract with this long-range research missile which uses advanced air-breathing propulsion to maintain full speed and manoeuvrability all the way to the (ship) target. The four long inlet ducts contribute to body lift, steering being by rear control fins driven from signals by an active nose seeker. STM is expected to lead to the next-generation anti-ship stand-off missile. Test flights from

Walleye, AGM-62

Origin: Martin Marietta, USA.
Propulsion: None.
Dimensions: Length (I) 135in (3.44mm), (II) 159in (4.04m); body diameter (I) 12.5in (317mm) (II) 18in (457mm); span (I) 45.5in (1.16m), (II) 51in (1.3m).
Launch weight: (I) 1,100lb (499kg), (II) 2,400lb (1089kg).
Performance: Speed subsonic; range (I) 16 miles (26km), (II) 35 miles (56km).
Warhead: (I) 825lb (374kg), (II) based on Mk 84 bomb.
Users: Include Israel, USA.

An unpowered glide bomb with TV guidance, AGM-62 Walleye was developed from 1963 by the NOTS at China Lake, assisted from 1964 by the Naval Avionics Facility. Intended to overcome the aircraft-vulnerability hazard of visual radio-command ASMs, Walleye quickly proved successful, and in January 1966 Martin was awarded the first production contract. This was later multiplied, and in November 1967 the need for Walleye in SE Asia resulted in Hughes Aircraft being brought in as second-source. In 1969 the Navy described

this missile as "The most accurate and effective air-to-surface conventional weapon ever developed anywhere". Walleye I has a cruciform of long-chord delta wings with elevons, a gyro stabilized TV vidicon camera in the nose, and ram-air windmill at the tail to drive the alternator and hydraulic pump. The pilot or operating crew-member identifies the target, if necessary using aircraft radar, aims the missile camera at it, focusses it and locks it to the target using a monitor screen in the cockpit. The aircraft can then release the missile and turn away from the target, though it must keep the radio link with the missile. In theory the missile

strike at targets up to 400 miles (650km) away without suffering unacceptably high attrition. Numerous studies have been made, numerous high-level meetings held (notably at ministerial level in August/September 1981) and several industrial collaborative links (even if temporary) forged in order to get a programme started. There is clearly no uniform idea of what is wanted, and by late 1982 no programme had emerged.

April 1979 onwards have used an A-7 as launch aircraft.

Above: STM ready for flight in 1982 trials from Navy A-7.

should glide straight to the target, but the launch operator has the ability to break into the control loop and, watching his monitor screen, guide it manually into the target. In 1968 the Navy funded several developments—Update Walleye, Walleye II, Fat Albert and Large-Scale Walleye among them—which led to the enlarged Walleye II (Mk 5 Mod 4) for use against larger targets. In production by 1974, Walleye II was deleted from the budget the following year and replaced by the first procurement of ER/DL (Extended Range/Data-Link) Walleye II (Mk 13 Mod 0). The ER/DL system was originally planned in 1969 to allow a launch-and-leave technique at greater distance from the target, the missile having larger wings to improve the glide ratio, and the radio data-link allowing the operator to release the missile towards the target and then, when the missile was much closer, acquire the target on his monitor screen, focus the camera and lock it on. Operations in SE Asia showed that it would be preferable to use two aircraft, the first to release the Walleye (if possible already locked on the approximate target position) and then escape and the second, possibly miles to one side, to update the lock-on point and monitor the approach to the target. Since 1978 about 1,400 I and 2,400 II missiles have been converted to ER/DL.

Below: US Navy A-4F with centreline tank, outer-wing ECM jammer pods and two Walleyes.

Anti-Tank

Armoured vehicles can be engaged by high-velocity guns, low-velocity 'bazooka' rockets, plunging fire from mortars, upwards blast from mines and, with especial effectiveness, by anti-tank guided missiles. The latter stemmed from a German weapon of 1944 which was steered to its target by electrical signals transmitted along very fine but strong wires unrolled behind the speeding missile. This method has been used in the majority of all anti-tank guided missiles ever built, and it is still numerically the No 1 system.

It was realized almost 30 years ago that the helicopter would be an excellent platform for missile systems of this type. Over the past 15 years emphasis has swung on to development of auxiliary systems such as stabilized optical sights (often augmented by IR or other wavelengths) which can give a magnified target image at night or in bad weather. Amazingly belatedly, it is only in the past year or two that the sight system has been mounted on a tall mast above the rotor, thus allowing the helicopter to engage hostile forces while remaining almost entirely invisible behind natural cover. There is no great problem in arranging for its missiles to pop up over this screen of trees, rising ground or even buildings, and a mast-mounted sight (MMS) is one of the best ways to give a helicopter a chance of returning from a mission.

These horizontal-flying missiles kill the tank in

various ways. Most have a hollow-charge, or shaped-charge, warhead which ejects a jet of metal forwards at such fantastic speed that it punches clean through the layer(s) of armour. Some have a HEAT or HESH head, while one of several recent solutions is the SFF (self-forging fragment) which hurls a blob of metal with such force that it goes right through the armour on its kinetic energy alone. Bill, a Swedish missile, introduces a modification to the traditional technique in flying one metre above the line of sight and firing a shaped-charge warhead at 30° downwards to punch through the relatively light top armour.

Quite apart from traditional horizontal-trajectory missiles there are a growing number of anti-armour systems which attack from above. Most involve clouds of small charges called bomblets, some fitted with individual 'smart' guidance and in many cases having the ability to convert themselves into conventional mines should they fail to hit a tank. 'Smart' means laser homing, and alternative forms of guidance include IR and IIR and the new millimetre-wave radar technology introduced with the Wasp. Whatever guidance, sight system and warhead is used, the combination of modern schemes of armour, ECM, decoys, AA defences and bad visibility will make the anti-tank mission a very challenging one throughout the foreseeable future.

Left: Most widely used anti-tank missile is the Hughes Tow, here caught by high-speed camera leaving quad launcher of a TowCobra gunship helicopter.

Below: It is difficult to comprehend why it took so long for the sight to progress from the nose of helicopters via the cabin roof to above the rotor.

AT-2 Swatter

Origin: Soviet Union.
Propulsion: Single-grain solid motor with inclined lateral nozzles.
Dimensions: Length 35.5in (902mm); body diameter 5.9in (150mm); span 26in (660mm).
Weight: At launch 55lb (25kg).
Performance: Speed 335mph (540km/h), range up to 7,220ft (2200m).
Warhead: Hollow-charge, pierces 23.6in (600mm).
Users: All Warsaw Pact countries, Afghanistan, Egypt, Syria.

Bearing in mind that it was planned in the early 1960s and was in action in 1967 this second-generation anti-armour missile was a remarkable technical achievement, and it is still deployed in very large numbers. In particular it is often seen on the Mi-8 ('Hip-E') and Mi-24 ('Hind-A' and 'Hind-D') Soviet helicopters. It has a constant-diameter tubular body, with a blunt tail which before launch is connected to a multi-pin umbilical plug. The motor fires through diagonal upper and lower nozzles to accelerate the missile off a long rail launcher which in the case of helicopter installations is under the body. Four rear wings have roll-control elevons, and the missile homes on the heat of its target detected by a sensitive nose seeker, driving two canard

AT-3 Sagger

Origin: Soviet Union.
Propulsion: Boost motor with four diagonal nozzles, sustainer has central nozzle with jetevator TVC for steering.
Dimensions: Length 34in (860mm); body diameter 5in (120mm); span 18in (460mm).
Weight: At launch about 24.9lb (11.3kg).
Performance: Speed high subsonic; range 1,640-9, 840ft (500-3000m).
Warhead: Hollow charge, 6.6lb (3kg), pierces 23.6in (600mm).
Users: All Warsaw Pact countries plus Afghanistan, Algeria, Angola, Egypt, Ethiopia, Iraq, Jugoslavia, Libya, Mozambique, Syria, Uganda, Vietnam and Yemen.

During the Middle East war in October 1973 two-man teams of Egyptian infantry opened what looked like small suitcases and inflicted casualties on Israeli battle tanks the like of which had seldom been seen on any battlefield. Ever since, the little missile codenamed Sagger by NATO has been treated with great respect, though it is still a simple device with no tube launcher or any guidance other than optical sighting and wire command. Called Miliutka in the Soviet Union, it was first seen in a Moscow parade in May 1965. Since

then it has been seen on many army platforms and it is also the usual anti-armour missile for helicopter use for export customers, including Poland's SM-2 and the Mi-8 'Hip-F'. The Mi-24 'Hind-A' can carry this missile on its four outboard launchers, firing from the hover or at low forward speeds. The missile is accelerated by a boost motor just behind the warhead, and flies on a sustainer with jet-deflection steering. There are no aerodynamic controls, but the small wings can fold for packaging. A tracking flare is attached beside the body, and it is claimed that an operator can steer to 3,300ft (1000m) with unaided eyesight, and to three times this distance with the magnifying optical sight used in air platforms.

Right: The anti-tank missile called AT-3 Sagger by NATO has so far been seen in service on two sub-types of Mi-8 Hip and on the SM-2 light twin-turbine helicopter derived from the Mi-2 and produced at WSK-PZL-Swidnik, Poland, one of which is shown here. No sighting device has been visible on any AT-3 carrier (some infantry missiles have been steered with the naked eye).

foreplanes, the missile rolling in bang/bang fashion to steer left/right. There are no guidance wires. Later missiles are only gradually replacing this prolific weapon.

Above: AT-2 Swatter fired from an Mi-24 Hind-D of Soviet Frontal Aviation. Normally a helicopter would stay at about one-tenth of this altitude.

AT-6 Spiral

Origin: Soviet Union.
Propulsion: Unknown type of rocket motor, probably dual-thrust solid.
Dimensions: Unknown, but length in region of 71in (1.8m); body diameter 5.5in (140mm).
Weight: Possibly about 70lb (32kg).
Performance: Speed about 620mph (1000km/h); range 150-16,500ft (50-5000m).
Warhead: Large HEAT (high-explosive anti-tank); penetrates at least 25.6in (650mm) at 90°.
Users: Most Warsaw Pact countries by 1983.

At first, in 1977 when it was first identified, this tube-launched system was believed to use the same missile as AT-4 and AT-5 but by 1980 Western observers had realized that it was completely new. Unlike other Soviet anti-tank missiles this has been identified only in air-launched applications, carried by the Mi-24 'Hind-E' and, it is believed, the Su-25 'Frogfoot' close-support attack aircraft. It homes on its target by laser guidance, the designator being either in the launch aircraft or aimed by friendly ground troops. The warhead is possibly of double-cone type and is judged able to knock out all known armour.

Right: Mi-24 'Hind-E' with outboard pylons for four AT-6 launch tubes, as well as four UV-32-57 rocket pods and the chin-position gun turret.

AT-X-?

Origin: Soviet Union.

During the past several years there has been a near-panic in NATO armies to find countermeasures against this supposed new anti-armour missile which has millimetre-wave guidance (like the Wasp, p.159). By late 1982 this missile appeared to be little more than a rumour based on the Soviet Union's known work on such radars.

Bantam, RB 53

Origin: AB Bofors, Sweden.
Propulsion: Bofors dual-thrust solid motor.
Dimensions: Length 33.4in (848mm); body diameter 4.3in (110mm); span 15.75in (400mm).
Weight: At launch 16.75lb (7.6kg).
Performance: Speed 188mph (303km/h); range 820-6,562ft (250-2000m).
Warhead: Hollow-charge Bofors, 4.2lb (1.9kg).
Users: Sweden, Switzerland.

Developed almost entirely by AB Bofors as a private venture from 1956, this is one of the smallest and lightest first-generation anti-tank missiles, and was notable for introducing a GRP airframe with folding wings to fit a slim container/launcher. In its simplest form for infantry the whole system, with one missile, weighs 44.0lb (20kg), with 66ft (20m) of cable to link the

Right: Training launch of a Bantam from an Agusta-Bell AB 204 (licensed 'Huey') helicopter of the Swedish Army light aviation units.

operator and launcher. If necessary the operator can add another 328ft (100m) of cable. Bantam has been fired from light aircraft such as the SK61 Bulldog and Saab Supporter and Agusta-Bell 204 helicopter. On leaving the launch box the wings flip open, their curved trailing-edge tips rolling the missile so that it can be steered by the trailing-edge spoilers sequenced by a pellet-spun gyro. The hollow-charge warhead has electrical double-skin fuzing and can penetrate up to 19.7in (500mm). Sweden adopted Bantam as missile RB53 in 1963, and—despite having their indigenous Mosquito—Switzerland followed in 1967. Production continued until about 1978.

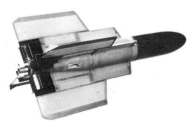

Left: Shown here with the four wings unfolded into the flight position, Bantam was one of the lightest and cheapest of the first-generation wire-guided anti-tank missiles. Steering was effected by the vibrating spoilers on the wing inboard trailing edges.

Hellfire

Origin: Rockwell International, USA.

Propulsion: Thiokol TX657 reduced-smoke 'all-boost' motor.

Dimensions: Length 64in (1626mm), body diameter 7in (178mm).

Weight: At launch 98.86lb (44.84kg).

Performance: Speed, quickly builds to Mach 1.17, range 'far in excess of present anti-armour systems'.

Warhead: Firestone 20lb (9kg) 7in-diameter hollow charge.

User: USA (Army, initially).

A direct descendent of Rockwell's Hornet, this missile has applications against hard point targets of all kinds, though it is officially described as "the USA's next-generation anti-armor weapon system". Numerous development firings took place from 1971 before full engineering go-ahead was received in October 1976. It has semi-active laser homing with a very advanced seeker from Martin Marietta. The seeker has a Cassegrain telescope under the hemispherical glass nose sending signals to the electronics section with micro-processor logic. Steering is by four canard controls, and Hellfire can pull 13g at Mach 1.17. The US Under-Secretary of Defense, the Hon. William J. Perry, said "This missile most

often goes right through the center of the bull's eye". The primary carrier is the AH-64A Apache helicopter (16 rounds) but Hellfire has flown on the Cobra and the A-10A Thunderbolt II fixed-wing platform. Numerous Hellfires have been launched without prior lock-on, some of them in rapid-fire homing on different multiple targets using ground designators with individual coding. The missile notices the laser radiation in flight, locks-on and homes at once. IOC will now be 1984, by which time this missile will probably also be developed with "launch-and-leave" IIR guidance. The first 680 rounds are being delivered before September 1984.

Right upper: First test firing of a Hellfire took place from an AH-1 Cobra of the US Army, at Redstone Arsenal. Hellfire is not expected to arm Army Cobras, but those of the Marine Corps may carry it.

Right: Main carrier of Hellfire will be the Army AH-64A Apache.

Below: This cutaway of Hellfire shows some of the unique features of this neat laser-homing anti-armour missile. The warhead jet goes through the guidance head.

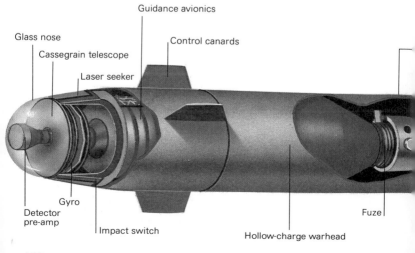

Guidance avionics

Glass nose

Cassegrain telescope

Control canards

Laser seeker

Gyro

Detector pre-amp

Impact switch

Fuze

Hollow-charge warhead

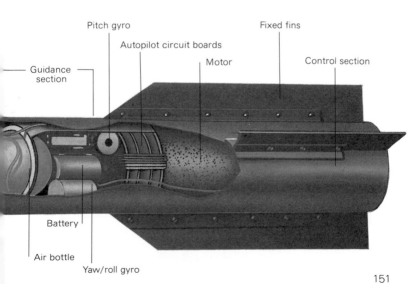

Guidance
section

Pitch gyro

Autopilot circuit boards

Motor

Fixed fins

Control section

Battery

Air bottle

Yaw/roll gyro

Hot

Origin: Euromissile GIE, France/Germany.
Propulsion: SNPE Bugeat boost and Infra cast double-base (Epictète) sustainer.
Dimensions: Length 50.2in (1275mm); body diameter (max, warhead/guidance) 6.5in (165mm); span (wings extended) 12.3in (312mm).
Weight: At launch 55.1lb (25kg).
Performance: Speed 560mph (900km/h); range 1,310-13,125ft (400-4000m).
Warhead: Hollow-charge 13.2lb (6kg).
Users: Egypt, France, West Germany, Iraq, Kuwait, Libya, Saudi Arabia, Spain, Syria and two unnamed customers.

This missile should really be Hottt (the name is often written all in capitals), because it is Hautsubsonique Optiquement Téléguidé Tiré d'un Tube—high-subsonic optical remote-guided fired from a tube. Work began with joint Franco-German army requirements, studies by Nord and Bölkow in 1964, engineering development and prolonged firing trials by Aérospatiale/MBB (which jointly formed Euromissile) and the start of mass production in 1977. Each missile is delivered as a round of ammunition in a sealed GRP tube.

The ignition signal fires the thermal battery, gyro and flares, gas pressure blowing the end-caps off the tube. The booster then fires inside the tube, burning for 0.9 sec and accelerating the missile to the speed given in the data; the sustainer then takes over and maintains this speed over a further 17.4 sec burn, giving times of 8.7 sec to 6,562ft (2000m), 12.5 sec to 9,842ft (3000m) and 16.3 sec to 13,123ft (4000m). The sustainer exhausts centrally where a single TVC spoiler can steer the missile. About 100-165ft (30-50m) from the launcher the safety system is deactivated to allow the sensitive fuze to detonate the head as soon as the streamlined nose skin is distorted. Penetration is 28in (700mm) at 0° and 11in (280mm) at 65°. Hot is in service with the Federal German Army BO 105P helicopter with six launch tubes, and Spain uses the BO 105C. France will have 160 SA.342M Gazelles, with four tubes each, as do several export customers. The SA.361H and various twin-engined Dauphin versions can carry eight, as does the Lynx, in all cases with stabilized magnifying night sights. Production of dawn-to-dusk systems proceeds at 800 rounds per month, but development and integration of night FLIR sights is a matter of urgency. Germany has adopted a TI system made under licence, while France uses a derivative of the SAT/TRT Thermidor.

Below: Demo of prototype Hot/Gazelle system at Camp de Mailly in 1973. The roof-mounted sight has a red rear fairing.

Above: Standard German Army anti-tank helicopter (PAH-1), the BO 105P carries six Hot tubes (only five here).

Below: Another view of the firing shown on the facing page. Wings have unfolded and the sustainer ignited.

MAF

Origin: Consortium led by OTO Melara, Italy.
Propulsion: SNIA Viscosa dual-thrust solid motor.

Dimensions: Not disclosed.
Weight: At launch 35.3lb (16kg).
Performance: Similar to TOW, p.156.

RBS 56 Bill

Origin: AB Bofors, Sweden.
Propulsion: Dual-thrust solid motor.
Dimensions: Not disclosed.
Weight: With firing container about 35lb (16kg).
Performance: Speed 450mph (725km/h); range limited to 6,560ft (2000m).
Warhead: Shaped charge directing jet downwards at at 30°.
User: Not yet adopted.

Right: Warhead detonation above a dummy tank.

Bofors undertook to develop this missile in mid-1979, sharing costs 50/50 with the Swedish FMV (official material administration). The name is the Swedish word for a pick (which penetrates); it is also an acronym for Bofors Infantry Light and Lethal. Though the immediate application is for ground troops, RBS 56 also has applications in helicopters and light aeroplanes. The design objective began with a warhead that would defeat any armour envisaged for the rest of the century, accepting penalties in range in order to keep the system light, simple and cheap. A novel feature is that Bill flies 39in (1m) above the line of sight so that it passes close above the enemy vehicle; a proximity fuze triggers the downwards-inclined warhead. Firings began in April 1981, with full development missiles being due for test from mid-1982 to late 1983. A production decision is expected in 1984.

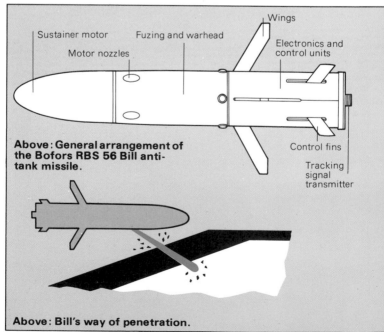

Sustainer motor
Motor nozzles
Fuzing and warhead
Wings
Electronics and control units
Control fins
Tracking signal transmitter

Above: General arrangement of the Bofors RBS 56 Bill anti-tank missile.

Above: Bill's way of penetration.

Warhead: Similar to TOW, p.156.
User: Not yet adopted (late 1982)

MAF (Missile Anti-carro Fanteria) is a private venture which completed a series of test firings in 1981-2 and by mid-1982 was being studied by the Italian army, with the A109A and A129 as possible helicopter platforms (its main role will be with ground troops). A laser beam-rider, it has a lightweight launcher, sight, telescope and laser by Officine Galileo. Another partner is Breda Meccanica.

Spark

Origin: United Technologies (Norden and CSD), USA.
Propulsion: CSD advanced solid-propellant ramjet.
Dimensions: Length 65in (1650mm); diameter 6.5in (165mm); fin span 10.5in (267mm).
Weight: Not stated.
Performance: Speed 'between Mach 3 and Mach 10'.
Warhead: Rod penetrator, no explosive.
User: US (Army) interest.

Spark (Solid-Propellant, Advanced Ramjet, Kinetic energy) is one of several programmes aimed at driving an anti-tank missile so fast it needs no warhead. The project was launched by the US Army Missile Command in September 1978. The projectile is a free-flying ramjet vehicle with a four-spoke solid boost rocket grain and a tubular solid ramjet fuel grain, giving high acceleration to a hypersonic (about Mach 5-6) speed which is sustained all the way to the target. The body is lined with Inconel alloy and there is room in the forebody for laser beam-riding guidance. The penetrator could be a rod of depleted uranium or other very dense material. The first Spark was successfully fired in September 1981, and several ground and helicopter firings have taken place since.

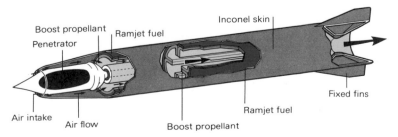

Boost propellant   Ramjet fuel   Inconel skin
Penetrator

Air intake   Air flow   Boost propellant   Ramjet fuel   Fixed fins

Tow, BGM-71

Origin: Hughes Aircraft, USA.
Propulsion: Hercules K41 boost
(0.05s) and sustain (1s) motors.
Dimensions: Length 45.75in
(1162mm); body diameter 6in
(152mm); span (wings extended)
13.5in (343mm).
Weight: At launch (BGM-71A)
46.1lb (20.9kg).
Performance: Speed 623mph
(1003km/h); range 1,640-12,300ft
(500-3750m).
Warhead: (BGM-71A) Picatinny
Arsenal 8.6lb (3.9kg) shaped-
charge with 5.3lb (2.4kg) explosive.
See text for later.
Users: Include Canada, Denmark,
Ethiopia, West Germany, Greece,
Iran, Israel, Italy, Jordan, Jugoslavia,
South Korea, Kuwait, Lebanon, Luxem-
burg, Morocco, Netherlands, Norway,
Oman, Pakistan, Saudi Arabia, Spain,
Sweden, Taiwan, Turkey, UK, US
(Army, Marines), Vietnam.

Often written TOW (Tube-launched,
Optically tracked, Wire-guided), this
weapon is likely to set an all-time
record in the field of guided-missile
production.

Prime contractor Hughes Aircraft
began work in 1965 to replace the
106mm recoilless rifle. The missile's
basic infantry form is supplied in a
sealed tube which is clipped to the
launcher. The missile tube is attached
to the rear of the launch tube, the
target sighted and the round fired. The
boost charge pops the missile
from the tube, firing through lateral
nozzles amidships. The four wings
indexed at 45° spring open forwards,

and the four tail controls flip open
rearwards. Guidance commands are
generated by the optical sensor in
the sight, which continuously mea-
sures the position of a light source in
the missile relative to the LOS and
sends steering commands along twin
wires. These drive the helium-pres-
sure actuators working the four tail
controls in pairs for pitch and yaw.
In 1976 production switched to ER
(Extended-Range) Tow with the
guidance wires lengthened from
9,842ft (3000m) to the figure given.
Sight field of view reduces from 6°
for gathering to 1.5° for smoothing
and 0.25° for tracking. The missile
electronics pack is between the motor
and the warhead.

Tow reached IOC in 1970, was
used in Vietnam and the 1973 Middle
East war, and has since been produced
at a higher rate than any other
known missile. The M65 airborne
Tow system equips the standard
American attack helicopter, the
AH-1S TowCobra and the Marines'
twin-engine AH-1J and -1T Improved
SeaCobra, each with a TSU Tele-
scopic Sight Unit) and two quad
launchers. Other countries use Tow
systems on the BO 105, Lynx,
A109, A129, 500MD and other
attack helicopters.

Hughes has developed a mast-
mounted sight (MMS) which uses
the BAe Tow roof sight but with a TV
down-tube, the whole mounted above
the rotor hub of the 500MD. In late
1981 production began of the Improved Tow, with a new warhead
triggered by a long probe, extended

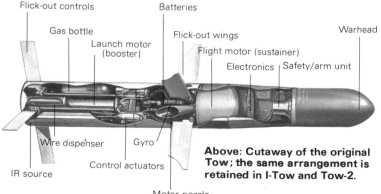

Flick-out controls · Batteries · Gas bottle · Flick-out wings · Warhead · Launch motor (booster) · Flight motor (sustainer) · Electronics · Safety/arm unit · Wire dispenser · Gyro · IR source · Control actuators · Motor nozzle

**Above: Cutaway of the original
Tow; the same arrangement is
retained in I-Tow and Tow-2.**

after launch to give 15in (381mm) stand-off distance for greater armour penetration. The shaped-charge head, with LX-14 filling and a dual-angle deformable liner, is also being retrofitted to many existing rounds. By late 1982 Hughes was near mass-production of Tow 2, which has several I-Tow improvements plus a new head with the same diameter as the rest of the missile with a mass of 13lb (5.9kg) and an even longer (21.25in, 540mm) extensible probe, calculated to defeat all tanks of the 1990s. Flight performance is maintained by a new double-base motor giving about 30 per cent greater total impulse. Both new missiles are for air-launch applications. By 1983 Tow output exceeded 320,000.

Right: The first live firing of Tow 2, in 1981, showing the ignition of the flight motor (sustainer); the probe, wings and control fins are all out.

Above: The three main members of the Tow family are (left) Tow, (centre) I (Improved) Tow and (right) the new Tow 2. The latter has a 6in (152mm) warhead with longer extensible probe; it also has a higher-impulse flight motor and new guidance to cope with hostile battlefield environments.

Trigat

Under this name, derived from tri (third) generation anti-tank, various European manufacturers are studying prospects for a new missile to incorporate technology suitable for the post-1990 period. Many warhead forms are being evaluated, but most studies revolve around IIR homing guidance on the target's thermal emissions, using staring focal-plane array seekers with electronic scanning and digital microprocessing. Leaders in the UK are BAe Dynamics and Mullard, but informal talks have been held with possible continental partners, especially Aérospatiale and MBB within the EMDG (Euromissile Dynamics Group) consortium.

WAAM

Origin: Various company studies, USA.

Since the late 1970s the WAAM (Wide-Area Anti-armor Munitions) programme has been the greatest part of the USAF's largest basic research effort into future tactical weapons. It runs parallel to the USA's Tank Breaker, which—though airborne sensors and illuminators play a major role—is for missiles fired from ground launchers. WAAM, often written and spoken Waam, comprises the Wasp missile (discussed separately, p.159), ERAM (Eram) and ACM. Eram, Extended-Range Anti-armor Mine, is an ambitious programme in which—at least until mid-1982—Honeywell and Avco were in competition. Most of the proposals are classified but in spring 1982 Avco was permitted to reveal its Skeet submunition, part of the Eram effort, clusters of which are carried in the USAF SUU-65 dispenser, as well as in the Vought T-22 Assault Breaker bus vehicle. Each Skeet warhead comprises a cylindrical body with four curved stabilizer fins flicked open as the payload is separated from the delivery vehicle. At the same time an offset unstreamlined mass called a wobble arm is extended from one side of the body, causing an oscillating motion which makes the IR sensor in the nose sweep over an area 'the size of a US football field'. A microprocessor converts images into steering commands until the warhead is directly over an armoured vehicle, whereupon the warhead fires straight down through the thin top armour. The transverse disc of explosive accelerates a lens of dense metal ahead of it so violently it is converted into an SFF (self-forging fragment) with a streamlined shape moving at some 9,000ft/s (2750m/s) to pass straight through the armour. Any warhead failing to acquire a target switches itself either into a low-altitude airburst mode or into a run-over mine lying on the ground.

Right: Last missile in this book, Wasp is also one of the cleverest and most compact. It remains to be seen to what extent such weapons can be procured in quantities large enough to permit speculative firing at unseen targets.

Below: Hughes engineer with usual screwdriver called for in publicity photos 'adjusts' Wasp's 94 GHz radar.

Wasp

Origin: Hughes Aircraft, USA.
Propulsion: Solid boost motor with 1s burn through central nozzle; two solid sustainers with diagonal lateral nozzles, fired in sequence.
Dimensions: (approximate) Length 59in (1.5m); body diameter 8in (203mm); span (wings and fins when extended) about 20in (508mm).
Weight: At launch 105lb (48kg).
Performance: Speed (constant) high subsonic; range several miles/km.
Warhead: Hollow charge of full forebody diameter firing jet through central hole in electronics/ guidance unit.
User: US (AF).

By far the most advanced in timing of the various USAF WAAM (see above) research programmes, Wasp progressed to an industrial competition between Hughes and Boeing which was won by the former in March 1982. Described as "The first ASM ever developed with the ability to identify and aim itself at tactical targets" Wasp fills the vital requirement of being cheap enough to deploy in swarms (hence the name) in a fire-and-forget mode while the launch aircraft stays safely out of sight behind a hill and away from the land battle area. The missile

has a classic configuration with large delta wings and rear rectangular control fins, but with the difference that all surfaces flick open after firing from a launch tube. The standard launcher is about the size of a 370-US gal drop tank, weighing almost 2,000lb (900kg). It has six tubes, each loaded with two missiles. That in the rear of each tube is protected by an exhaust deflector which diverts the boost-motor blast of that in front out through side ports. Clear of the tube, the missile climbs from treetop height to its cruise altitude at a steady high speed. It levels off and its millimetre-wave (94GHz) pulsed radar seeker sweeps up to 45° off-axis looking for metal targets. Trials with the homing head mounted in a pod under a Sabreliner at Eglin AFB in 1982 "showed that the seeker repeatedly found the targets while flying over strong ground clutter". All 12 rounds in a pod can be fired in 2s. The F-16 normally carries two pods, as can the Harrier, Jaguar, Mirage 5 and Alpha Jet; the F-111, A-10 and Tornado would normally carry four. Flight testing began in November 1982, and the programme has been so successful a production decision could be taken in late 1983.

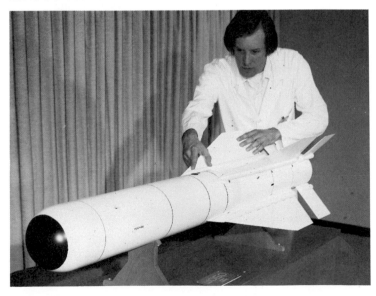

OTHER SUPER-VALUE MILITARY GUIDES IN THIS SERIES......

OTHER ILLUSTRATED MILITARY GUIDES NOW AVAILABLE...

Allied Fighters of World War II
Bombers of World War II
German, Italian and Japanese Fighters of World War II
Modern Fighters and Attack Aircraft
Modern Soviet Navy

Modern Submarines
Modern Tanks
Modern US Navy
Modern Warships
Pistols and Revolvers
Rifles and Sub-Machine Guns
World War II Tanks

* Each has 160 fact-filled pages
* Each is colourfully illustrated with hundreds of action photographs and technical drawings
* Each contains concisely presented data and accurate descriptions of major international weapons
* Each represents tremendous value

If you would like further information of any of our titles please write to:

Publicity Dept. (Military Div.), Salamander Books Ltd.,
27 Old Gloucester Street, London WC1N 3AF

PRINTED IN BELGIUM BY

INTERNATIONAL BOOK PRODUCTION